A CPAS handbook

UNDER FIVES AND THEIR FAMILIES

Judith Wigley

Series editor Paul Simmonds

Cartoons by Roy Mitchell

MarshallPickering

An Imprint of HarperCollins*Publishers*

Marshall Pickering
An imprint of HarperCollins*Publishers*
77–85 Fulham Palace Road
Hammersmith, London W6 8JB

First published in Great Britain in 1990
by Marshall Pickering

9 8 7 6 5 4 3 2

A catalogue record for this book
is available from the British Library

Printed in Great Britain by
HarperCollinsManufacturing, Glasgow

UNDER FIVES AND THEIR FAMILIES

Contents

*Parent and toddler groups are informal community groups which aim
to provide a relaxed atmosphere and safe play environment where
parents and pre-school children can enjoy meeting.*

CHAPTER TWO – Christian Playgroups   43

Playgroups are not part of the statutory pre-school educational requirements but are legally registered voluntary groups set up by trained volunteers concerned for the development of children aged between two and a half and five years. Whilst parents play an important part in the running of groups, they do not remain with their child during a playgroup session.

PART TWO   **Children in the Church**   59

Introduction – Children and God   61

CHAPTER THREE – Pram Services   67

Pram Services are informal midweek services that aim to introduce pre-schoolers and their parents to the Christian faith and worship.

This chapter identifies and discusses some of the difficulties encountered by under fives in Sunday services of worship. Practical suggestions are offered as positive means of welcoming, involving and including young children as part of the worshipping body of Christ.

The sharing of our faith is an integral part of the sharing of our lives in everything we say and do. But it can also take place within an organised event or group set up for that specific purpose. This chapter looks at three different ways of setting up such events and the practicalities of leading them.

The task of supporting one another is the responsibility of everyone. This chapter suggests practical ways of praying together, leading, and enlisting the support of church leaders and members.

This chapter gives details of procedures and suppliers of books, leaflets, magazines and audio-visual aids, and the names of supportive organisations and groups, all of which provide useful sources for under fives groups.

Foreword

It is interesting to reflect on the fact that over the last ten years or so work amongst the under fives and their parents has become one of the fastest growing areas in the lives of many churches. There are many reasons for this.

Churches have found that their Playgroups and Toddler groups have been warmly welcomed by local communities; young mums are often quite isolated and many have found in the churches an acceptance and an understanding that has helped them along the way. They have also found friendship and support, and some have found faith as well.

The Churches themselves have been blessed: not only have they been of real service to the community, they have also found that their own members have been able to speak about their faith in a context that is authentic to them. Noise, crises, chicken pox, baby-sitters, more noise, family concerns and the rest provide such a context in which people can discover, experience and commend their faith.

Many of these groups for under fives and their parents were started with more enthusiasm than experience; it is a good way to learn but reading about how other groups are organised can be a real tonic. I believe that at last we now have a book which can interest us, instruct and inspire us. It is both a story and a manual, and I have great confidence in commending it to you.

Judith Wigley writes from her own experience, much of it in this diocese. Like many others she started off 'in the deep end' and it was a case of sink or swim; fortunately she swam, and survived to pass on all sorts of helpful insights. In reflecting on her experiences over the past ten years, she has been selective, and gathered her material together in a way which will be of enormous help to a great many others who are 'standing at the waters' edge'.

Judith's experience, style and integrity mean that she is in considerable demand at conferences and workshops on this theme, and she is most definitely not one of those people who have been driven to print because they cannot cope in practice!

This book is the first in a new series of practical guides from CPAS. I hope that it will help many churches to get started, and I commend it to any who want to work with the under fives and their parents.

† Robert Bradford

Preface

There were times when I would have gladly locked myself in the boiler house in order to escape the noise and chaos. I was quite prepared for a challenge. But this was proving very noisy, messy and incredibly hard work. It certainly wasn't like anything I'd been used to — no time for cosy chats with the other leaders except as you carried the climbing frame up from the boiler room, each gripping one end of the slide hoping that you wouldn't push the other headlong down the stone steps.

I felt thrown in at the deep end not realising at the time that there was no shallow end. I was only temporarily helping out at the toddler group whilst I settled down into parish life, having just married the vicar. That was eleven years ago. Here I am today still working with the under fives and their families.

Not even the boiler house steps could prevent me from seeing the glaring needs of these families and the gap that existed between them and the church. What went on inside the building on a Sunday had little relevance to the midweek occupants. And many of these families weren't even aware that the building opened on Sundays. The only thing that the two groups of people had in common was literally the ground that they walked on.

Here was our challenge. Somehow we had to bridge that gap. We had to discover ways and means of demonstrating and declaring the love of God. The majority weren't interested so it wasn't a case of simply telling them — they'd soon disappear from our sight. We had a lot to learn. Most of all we learnt of the privileges and opportunities in working through under fives

groups. Privileges and opportunities that every church family
can find. On every church's doorstep is a community of parents
and young children, especially children who are under five.

When I first started working with under fives groups I was
desperate for help, encouragement and ideas. I could find
nothing. Now things are improving and I hope this book will
help. Many of the guidelines and suggestions are practical. But
I've also tried to deal with some of the issues that emerge. I
hope that it will encourage you in your work or help you to
support and encourage those in your church who are already
doing it.

Part One
FAMILIES IN
THE COMMUNITY

Introduction — The Opportunity to Serve, Share and Challenge

As Christians we spend a lot of time talking about how we can reach out into the community around us with the message of God's love. Some of us are engaged in open youth clubs, luncheon clubs for the elderly, or well organised home visiting programmes. A lot of time, energy and finance can be ploughed into these valuable activites. What puzzles me is why the church has been so slow to recognise some of the most obvious and potentially exciting channels for reaching families — under fives groups.

Under fives groups bring the church into contact with not just children but parents, extended families, outside agencies working with families and the community at large. The influence we can have upon the lives of these people is far reaching. The opportunities are great and I'd like to share some of them with you at the beginning of this section.

We have the opportunity to *serve*

There are very few young families in our country that don't attend some kind of pre-school community group. A lot of these groups have replaced the support and companionship once found in the extended family unit — a structure upon which our communities used to be built. Sociological changes since the war have resulted in fewer natural family and extended family support structures and consequently a rise in the need for other groups where parents and children can meet together and find in each other many of the resources they need. Play centres, day nurseries, playgroups, parent and toddler groups and parent support groups are just some of the ways in which churches can serve the needs of their local communities. By far the most common are parent and toddler groups and playgroups.

This kind of service is not offered as a public relations exercise for the church. It is the outworking of ordinary Christian lives following the example of Jesus. It is the offering of support, care, compassion and hope found in the message of the cross. It is expressing the love of Christ in action.

It is also a way of influencing the quality of life in our communities. Some of the most exciting work amongst young families in our cities is being carried out through the vision and hard work of Christians from local churches. Other agencies are recognising this commitment and many have joined forces working together for the good and wellbeing of the world in which they live. Of course it is a costly business in terms of time, energy, money and prayer but it is an open opportunity to serve and influence our communities with the message of the kingdom of God.

We have the opportunity to *share*
Large numbers of under fives groups are set up by Christian women with the prime intention of sharing with others their faith in Christ. The informal surroundings of such groups provide every opportunity for building up friendships and the sharing of our whole lives — central to which will be our faith. The common interests and experiences of parents are an excellent basis for this sharing.

The time between the birth of a baby into a family and full-time education is one of those periods in life when parents are open to thinking about their lives, what, if anything, life means, and the direction in which they are going. The first-time responsibility of new parents often weighs heavily upon them and feelings of inadequacy and searching questions surface fast. They realise that their children look to them for spiritual as well as moral and practical guidelines for living. Many, I believe, are open to listening and considering the faith that we have to share.

The sharing of our lives with these families is a vital stage in what can sometimes seem to be a long process. But God is at work here as much as he is at any other stage.

We have the opportunity to *challenge*.

At first the opportunity to challenge families in under fives groups with the message of the cross may seem very distant. Many will have little understanding of what we are presenting. The gap between the families entering our groups and the message we want to offer could be very big. Our serving and sharing may go on for years before we feel we have the opportunity to challenge. It is rare for a family which simply attends the playgroup to respond immediately to, say, an invitation to a guest service. (There are exceptions as in the case of the young mother attending a toddler group who came to faith as a direct result of a leader offering to pray for her sick child.) The path taken from initial contact to challenge resulting in faith and commitment will vary for each person.

The time and place for that challenge will vary also. It may come from a friend as the result of on-going witness at a one-to-one level. For many it will undoubtedly come during baptism or dedication preparation, small group work, a major faith-sharing event that the whole church may organise or through a particular Sunday service. In our previous church it was interesting to watch the increasing emphasis on the morning service as we saw an increase in family contacts, including the many men linked to the women attending the groups. It is exciting to see whole families challenged with the message of the cross and saying, 'I turn to Christ.'

It is a *family* work

The whole of this work is centred on the family. In every kind of under fives group we are meeting and influencing whole families. Where else in the life of our churches except through our own personal contacts with friends and neighbours do we have this privilege and opportunity? There comes a stage when children attend groups independently of their parents or vice versa. Then we begin to try to reach the parents through the children or children through the parents. It's hard work. However at the pre-school age we find them together and at a stage when they are open to what we have to share with them.

The family is an important part of the order created by God. It is in and through the relationships within the family that God chose to reflect his nature and character. In working with families we are in effect restoring the image of God as he chose to reveal it. It is a powerful force and we are engaged in front-line work for the kingdom of God. It won't be easy. We will sometimes have a fight on our hands against 'sin, the world and the devil'. But it is I believe an opportunity and challenge to which the church as a whole should respond.

There are thousands of under fives community groups up and down the country engaged in the work of serving, sharing and challenging, but many exist as a drainpipe attachment to their churches. They are viewed with suspicion and are given little backing in terms of prayer, time or finance. There appears to be an inability to see beyond the messy activity, noise, hard work and cost that accompany a work of this kind.

Two of the most commonly found groups are parent and toddler groups and playgroups. It is these two that I want to consider in the first part of this book.

1
Parent and Toddler Groups

Parent and toddler groups are informal community groups which aim to provide a relaxed atmosphere and safe play environment where parents and pre-school children can enjoy meeting.

Last year the BBC produced a programme called 'Who'd marry a vicar?' It portrayed several vicars' wives living in mansion-style vicarages doing what the average person's expectation of a conventional role would be. It was awful, and for me and many others it did absolutely nothing for our already suspect image! The day following the showing of this programme a mum who had attended our toddler group a few years previously stopped me and asked if I had watched it.

'Well,' she said, 'I told my husband that our vicar's wife is not like that, or our church. They get out and get involved, not sit in their mansions drinking tea!'

This mum had never come to anything other than the toddler group, and in fact refused every invitation to discussion groups, services or any special event that we laid on. But here she was claiming me and the church as hers! She had obviously identified with God's people and knew that she had access to them through her contacts at toddlers group. I guess I had considered her to be one of our 'failures', one of the untouched, but this conversation taught me never to underestimate what God is doing in people's hearts and minds. I knew that in the day when she needed God or the comfort of his people, she would not be afraid of looking for it and would know just where to come. All this was because of the work of one small parent and toddler group.

1.1 What is a parent and toddler group?

Parent and toddler groups vary considerably in their size, structure, content, aims and objectives but their common feature lies in the age group of children that attend and the fact that parents (mostly mothers) remain with their children. The age of the children can be from birth to five years, but in areas where nursery and playgroup provision is good the majority are between birth and three years. Parent and toddler groups arise out of a need for children and parents to meet together in a safe and relaxed environment.

Few groups are actually called Parent and Toddlers. Many select their own names in order to convey a more attractive image, for example, Thursday Break, Rainbow Club, and even Squeels on Wheels. Such titles do not exclude the increasing number of dads, grannies, childminders or guardians that may benefit from attending.

1.2 Who runs a parent and toddler group?

There are, of course, many groups formed by caring parents concerned for their local community. Town or community halls are often used as a base but more frequently churches are sought for their large halls and classrooms which lie vacant between Monday and Friday. Clergy and ministers are usually glad to see the buildings put to good use and come to an agreement on a suitable rent to cover heat, light, and wear and tear. It is unusual for the church leaders or members to have any further involvement in the running of such community groups.

However there is no doubt that change is in the air. An increasing number of Christians are becoming aware of the opportunities found in parent and toddler groups for sharing their faith. The enlightened folk are not necessarily the clergy and ministers, more often it is the Christian mums themselves who begin to see the openings. Where a group already exists on their church premises they are seeking to get involved and create these opportunities. Of course this can often be a slow process if unsympathetic people are in control but nonetheless they make that effort. Increasingly, where a group does not exist, a specifically Christian group is being started. There is a definite awakening to the potential of this whole field of ministry.

1.3 Establishing the aims of a Christian group

It is important to discuss and establish from the start the aims of a Christian parent and toddler group. One of my husband's favourite sayings is, 'If we aim at nothing, we'll hit it!' (Think about it — it's true.) It may even help to write down the agreed aim. For example, we may decide, 'Our aim is to demonstrate and declare the love of God to these families in showing and telling them how they can know God personally through Jesus Christ.'

We need to keep sight of that aim, that vision. It needs to be central to our praying especially as it could be some time before we see it fulfilled. We must try to maintain our sense of purpose and direction. I like to think that God calls us to be visionaries. He invites us to daydream with him.

I confess that I find daydreaming quite easy. I spent large chunks of my schooldays practising! Sometimes as I sat in our parent and toddler group I would imagine hundreds of parents pouring into church every day looking for friendships, care, concern and most of all looking for God. I dreamed of discussion groups, bible studies, creches and lives changed by the presence of God. Of course the reality was quite different, but often God takes and uses our dreams as the driving force behind what in practice is very hard work.

Part of our last parish was in an Urban Priority Area and in its early days the toddler group was crowded out with young mothers who appeared to want to do nothing but sit in small groups, smoke cigarettes and allow their toddlers to wander unattended. Leaders were few and I began to question the Lord as to how this could ever be considered a form of reaching out.

He reminded me of my dream to see mothers won for Christ and encouraged me to understand that our very presence alongside these mums was his presence. This was fact and not dependent on what we as leaders were feeling. Following that, each time I swept the floor or mopped up puddles of every description I would picture a candle in the dark — God's light shining out in the darkness. At such difficult times we need to hold on to the vision and calling that we first had and it is critical that we establish our aims at the start.

1.4   Short-term goals
Achieving our aim in parent and toddler groups is often a very long process. Many families entering our groups are a long way from God, with little knowledge or understanding of him or of Jesus as his son. Gone are the days when we could presume that everyone had a basic knowledge of Christianity. It was a great help to me in my early days of working with parents in toddler groups to understand some of the stages that people go through before coming to faith and commitment. These stages are often:

Awareness of the supernatural
Initial awareness of Christianity
Interest in Christianity
Awareness of basic facts of the gospel
Grasp of the implications of the gospel
Positive attitude to the gospel
Awareness of personal need
Challenge and decision to act
Repentance and faith
Commitment

This enabled me to set myself short-term goals, identifying some of these stages on the way. It also affected how we prayed. We prayed very specifically for increased spiritual awareness. We prayed that the little things like posters on the wall,

Christian birthday cards given to the children and Christian birth congratulation cards sent to mums would communicate some very basic facts about Christianity.

Basic things like learning names of parents, building up friendships, channelling the energies of difficult children, welcoming new parents all become important stages — important short-term goals. On occasions my own prayers and goals were extremely basic!

Some weeks after my arrival at the toddler group my identity as 'the vicar's wife' was revealed. One mother was none too pleased and saw my presence as a real threat to her cosy little gathering. In no uncertain terms she told me that if I dared to introduce anything religious into the group they'd all either boycott the place or mount a 'take-over' bid. I don't mind admitting that I was terrified of her — she was a very forceful and influential woman. I could well believe that the entire group would follow wherever she led. There was no alternative but to make her the subject of my daily prayers. If I was to have the courage to face her each week I needed all the divine help I could get.

My prayers and goals started with the things like, 'Dear Lord I pray that she might simply look at me this week without disdain and aggression in her face.' The following week it continued, 'Oh Lord, please help me to smile at her this week.' The third week: 'Oh Lord, please may we be able to simply acknowledge each other by saying "hello"!'

This continued for months and months until we really were communicating well. Neither of us could believe it. It had to be a miracle. The following year when we started to run discussion groups and were inviting people to guest services, not only was she amongst the first to come, but she made the others come, too!

1.5 Demonstrating God's love in practice
There are many in our groups like the parent just described.

They just don't want to know. To talk to them about Christianity would probably result in their leaving the group in fear of having religion pushed down their throats. There is a sense in which we have to earn our right to speak about our faith. We need to demonstrate God's love in our actions.

Showing God's love in practice will mean responding to the individual and corporate needs of the families who attend. Careful assessment of your local community will help here. It can be surprising just how many glaring needs go unnoticed until you begin to look for them.

The leaders of one Christian parent and toddler group in an Urban Priority Area went from door to door with a questionnaire inviting young families to state their greatest needs. After collating the results they set about the task of providing some of the practical things mentioned.

In a previous church we had a real mixture of people attending the parent and toddler group which in practice meant responding to a wide range of social, emotional and material needs. The Muslim lady with few words of spoken English, the single parent struggling to survive, the professional career-bound 'first time' mother desperate for adult contact during her maternity leave — all walked in through our doors each week.

Only a few hundred yards down the road from that church was another working entirely amongst Muslims and Hindus — their immediate locality is 95 per cent Asian in origin. The process of demonstrating God's love in practice was quite different. They had to learn about Asian faiths and cultures in order to understand their families. Some group leaders in multi-cultural areas even go as far as to learn another language! Showing love and concern to families of other faiths and cultures demands sensitivity and respect. We need to be made aware of our own hidden prejudices and seek to overcome them. Further discussion of some of these issues can be found in chapter 2.5.

Not all of us have to face the prospect of communicating in a foreign language. There are many obvious and practical ways in which we can respond to the needs around us.

Some suggestions are listed below.

Some practical suggestions for showing love and concern

Daytime babysitting circle to enable parents to attend hospital, dental, or any other important engagement

Shopper's creche to enable parents to do a weekly food shop alone

Crisis 'phone line for an emergency

Information on family support groups, e.g. Gingerbread, Relate, Step-parents Association, Samaritans

Up-to-date information on DSS benefits and allowances particularly for the unemployed and single parents

Children's and women's health information, e.g. immunisation, childhood illnesses, well women's clinics

Second-hand clothes stall for both parents and children

Toy, book, story audio-tape and video libraries for parents — secular and religious

Slimming and exercise group for parents

Hairdressing facilities for children during a group session

Social night out for parents

Summer day trip for families to the coast or a local attraction, especially for those who do not get a holiday

Holidays arranged for needy families, either with your church's financial support or through organisations like Mother's Union

Details of adult education courses, especially those run during the day with creche facilities

All of these communicate care and concern. Our actions need to do the speaking in the first instance and then we shall earn our right to speak about God.

1.6 Declaring God's love in word

Earlier in this chapter we acknowledged that we should avoid doing things that might create the impression that we are trying to push religion down people's throats. The right to share our faith should arise out of respect for, and friendships with, the parents. Does this mean that there is no place at all for speaking directly about Christ to the group other than on a one-to-one basis in private conversation?

Many groups feel that such a place can be created. But it needs to be planned and prepared with prayer and sensitivity. It requires careful thought and should not be treated lightly. There is a danger of causing more harm than good. In the past our own group has experienced a real division between those who joined in these times and those who didn't. Other groups have had very positive and encouraging responses. Much depends on the awareness of the parents to whom you are speaking and how willing they are to listen. Only you can decide what is right for your group.

There are basically two ways of approaching such an occasion. Either parents and children gather together for a joint session, or parents withdraw to another room and have their own group time, leaving someone in charge of the children. Whichever you consider, time is very limited. Thirty minutes is probably the maximum time available within an ordinary toddler group meeting. Anything longer will dominate the session and so change the nature of the whole group.

In considering either type of group ask three important questions:
• What is the best time in the programme for it?
• How do we encourage everyone to join in?
• What will the content be?

A time for parents and children together
The most suitable time is probably between the middle and the end of a session after the children have burnt off any excess energy. Some groups organise it as tea or coffee is being served, when there is naturally lots of movement enabling the rearrangement of chairs, etc.

Singing can be an excellent starter and provides the opportunity to introduce some of the many Christian songs and choruses. If you are not musical there is an increasing number of cassette tapes available for under fives (listed, in chapter 7.15). Some groups have had parents request a copy of the words of songs and choruses to take home and sing with their children. (I frequently smile to myself at the thought of dozens of children singing 'God's not dead, No! He's alive!' at bathtime each night.)

Birthdays can also be announced and suitably celebrated with a card and perhaps the gift of a small Christian book for children — that's if you can afford it. It also serves as a useful time to give out any important notices.

The main input may be the telling (not reading) of a Bible story using some of the wonderfully illustrated books that are now available. Whilst the whole time is geared to the children, the message is still relevant to the parents listening in. For those parents who have little or no knowledge of Christianity this is an important time of learning. Many will not have heard what we consider well known Bible stories. And the Bible is full of them so we're not in danger of running out of material. For some practical tips on storytelling see chapter 3.6. If your church is experienced in leading 'all age' worship you may well get some ideas and help from those responsible for the planning of these services.

Parents only
Obviously when parents leave, the children will need to be otherwise entertained, which requires many extra hands and careful planning. The programme of the adults' group needs to be brief, probably only twenty to thirty minutes at the most. This is long enough for someone to give a personal testimony or a short talk. It might include a Christian's experience of miscarriage, death, divorce, single parenting. Some groups use this time to cover important child-related subjects such as discipline, eating habits, children and baptism, etc. A mixture of social, health, educational and religious topics usually combines well. For further suggestions on topics see chapter 5.4.

If you bring in an outside speaker do tell them what to expect in terms of length of talk, numbers of mothers to expect and the likelihood of one or two children being present. They need to be well prepared.

Many audio-visual resources such as videos and audio-cassette tapes are too long for this type of gathering and most require some sort of discussion time if they are to be used to their full. They are more suited to a separate occasion set up for that specific purpose rather than squeezing them into the limited time available during a parent and toddler group session. Such faith sharing or teaching groups are easily organised as we shall discuss in a later chapter.

1.7 Practicalities — insurance

The key to an efficiently run parent and toddler group is careful advance planning and preparation. Poor organisation will only serve to weaken our Christian witness. We may not at first have all the practical resources that we feel are necessary, but an effort to make the most of what we do have will go a long way towards creating healthy and positive attitudes in the minds of those who attend.

One very important area that should not be overlooked is that of insurance cover. Few church insurance policies include the kind of cover that mid-week children's groups of this kind require. The Pre-School Playgroups Association offer an umbrella policy to all affiliated parent and toddler groups. It is a very good and reasonably priced policy.

1.8 Facilities

A church-based group will want, if possible, to use its own building. But there are groups who recognise their limitations and hire more suitable facilities but still retain their church base and Christian aims. There may be parts of your church building that have not previously been used for children's work but which you consider ideal, such as carpeted lounges. Take courage in your hands and approach the 'powers that be' and ask to use them. They can only say no.

We need to aim high at all times in the facilities we try to provide. It is amazing what can be done with a little imagination and professional advice. A friendly architect or builder may open up all sorts of possibilities and costs can always be reduced by using voluntary labour from church folk.

Facilities required for parent and toddler groups

Safety Every safety factor relevant to the home should be applied to the toddler group.

Storage Toys and equipment have a habit of growing! You will rarely have enough storage space. Both a lock-up cupboard and a storage area for larger items will be necessary.

Floor surfaces Remember the different needs of babies, crawlers and walkers. Designate messy areas, quiet areas, and run-around areas.

Toilet and washing You will need a nappy changing area, potties and trainer seats as well as hot water.

Kitchen Coffee and juice-making facilities must be high on the list of priorities.

1.9 Equipment

The quantity of toys and equipment required by a group will depend largely on numbers of children attending and the space — not least storage space. However there are various ways of acquiring these different things. You can beg (well, ask nicely), borrow or buy.

Obtaining equipment

Begging:
— Ask church members to donate suitable good quality toys or money to buy them. Don't be frightened to apply for grants from your local authorities. Try both your Town Hall (department of education) and Social Services and be prepared to persist to get through the red tape.

— for a very special need apply to BBC Children in Need Appeal.

Borrowing:
— books from the local library on a termly basis
— from families who won't need them until 'the next one'
— large equipment from toy or community libraries.

Buying:
— make use of local 'free' paper advertising
— second-hand school furniture is sometimes sold off by local education authorities
— discounts are offered to groups by specialist shops such as Early Learning and Galt Toys.
— PPA do 'bulk buy' sales for play and craft materials
— purchase larger items through wholesale catalogues not shops
Details of your local PPA and community toy libraries can usually be found at your local book library.

1.10 Finances
Careful handling of all finances not only helps the smooth running of a toddler group but it can also save you from financial embarrassnent. A record of income and expenditure along with receipts should be kept and this is best done by the same two people each week to save confusion and help continuity in money management. It will probably be necessary to open a bank account in the name of the group, and for this names of leaders need to be submitted and official forms signed. Give some consideration to the following areas.

Budgeting: Try to estimate the known areas of expense such as rent, administration costs, refreshments, membership of support groups such as PPA, insurance cover (PPA offer a good cover for toddler groups) and play materials.

Subscription: Work out a realistic subscription charge for those attending the group. This is always a debateable area and groups vary in their opinions. I think it is true to say that people will pay for a good service, especially when the costing out of their subscription is explained to them. Our own group always offered a subsidy for single parent families and those where both parents were out of work. I recently met a group who made no charge for the service they provided as a parent and toddler group. The church covered all expenses as part of their service to the community.

Fundraising: Expenditure nearly always outweighs income in parent and toddler groups and consequently the issue of fundraising inevitably surfaces. Many churches have strict policies about fundraising — they don't allow it. Some toddler groups themselves adopt a no fundraising policy, preferring to work within their limitations or depending on direct giving from Christians involved in the work. We have given considerable thought to this issue over the years and finally concluded that it was good in principle for parents to have some kind of responsibility towards the maintenance of the group. What we tried to avoid was a never-ending stream of events that conveyed the eternal message of 'we need money'. Our compromise was two events a year where we combined a social night with fundraising. It nearly always involved food of some description and as many different stalls as we could get. Mothers who were party plan reps brought their wares and others managed cake, clothing, craft, toy and many other types of stalls. A specific goal was always set for the evening such as the purchase of a new climbing frame or slide and trampoline. We also sought to give money away as an example of our concern for those less fortunate than ourselves. They were usually child-centred charities such as the NSPCC or local hospice projects.

Church support: Last but not least, do approach your church for financial help. They may not be able to give very much in a direct form but they may carry the cost of heat and light or reduce the rent. Every little helps and it may be worth pointing out that other church groups that meet on a Sunday (e.g. Sunday schools) often don't get charged for using the premises and probably receive grants for their resources. Check also if your church require you to submit your books for audit at the end of the financial year. Many do require this and it is better to know in advance so that everything is in order.

1.11 Publicity

The initial publicity for a group starting from scratch is important. A bright, cheerful and easily read poster will communicate far more than the basic information written on it. It saddens me to see small, tatty posters with letters so small they can barely be read. The image we convey to the general public matters, we need to make a real effort.

The most effective form of advertising is of course word of mouth. Midwives, health visitors, and doctors are always in contact with young families. Also, make the most of casual church contacts such as baptism enquirers, cradle rolls, and the casual family service attender. There are basically two types of paper publicity: the professionally produced and the DIY kind.

Professional: There are many 'instant print' shops around that will design and print cards and/or posters for you but they are expensive. The Christian Publicity Organisation is one of the biggest and best in the field of church publicity. They produce varying shapes, sizes and designs of cards, leaflets and posters suitable for nearly every type of church group including toddler groups. Blank picture cards can be bought for you to write on

WHALE OF A TIME
Boys and Girls
WEDNESDAY
ADVENTURE CLUB
STARTS AGAIN
7th September, 6 o'clock
at Ryhope Pentecostal Church
One hour of:
Games—Prizes—Singing
Stories—Competitions
FREE

Ref CPO 833. The black wording above is only
a suggestion to show how the card will look with
local wording on it. There is no pre-printed
wording. No poster available.

Reproduced by kind permission of *Christian Publicity Organisation*, Garcia
Estate, Canterbury Road, Worthing, West Sussex, BN13 1BW.

your own details. For a little extra cost there is an overprinting service. This takes longer and should be ordered well in advance. Appropriate logos can be printed onto plain cards and the same design posters can be bought to match many of these designs.

DIY: Don't despair! It is quite easy to do. The most useful aids are tracing paper, a photocopier and brightly coloured felt tip pens. If your church does not own its own photocopier look around your local shops and offices as there are usually plenty who are willing to loan the facility for a small price per copy. The majority of these machines now reduce and enlarge which means you can easily produce matching cards and posters for between three and ten pence. Choose a very simple design and even use stencils for the lettering. Colouring them in can be great fun. We regularly did ours at leaders' meetings as we talked.

Where do you place posters and cards? Simple! In every place where young families go! Doctors' surgeries, health centres, baby clinics, post offices, shops and supermarkets, to name but a few. Always ask permission before placing them and go armed with your own blue-tack, offering to hang them yourself. Some shops may ask for a small fee. Do keep an eye on them and replace them when necessary. If you can afford it, change the design once or twice a year as people grow immune to the same picture after a while. Even better, keep the basic design which will become the group's identity but change the layout of information.

1.12 Internal communication

Internal communication within a group is as important as the external publicity. When people join a group they like to know what they have come to, who is in charge, how much it costs, what happens and what is expected of them and their child. Think back to the last time you went anywhere new, perhaps a new job, the baby clinic, hospital, or even the theatre or cinema.

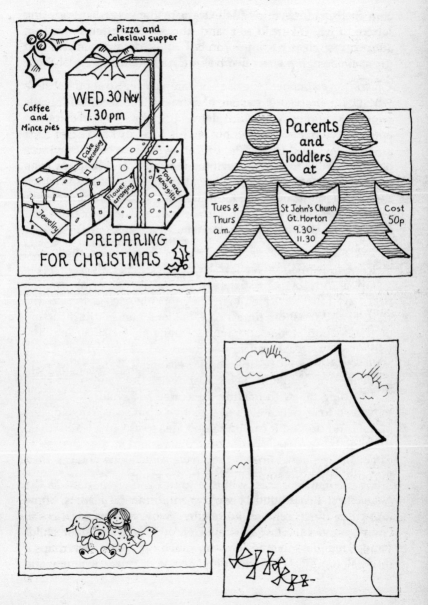

You probably looked for all the signs telling you what to do and where to go. We need to ensure that all important details are simply but clearly communicated to those who attend our groups. There are several ways of achieving this.

Efficient registration: Devise a simple registration system whereby you record names of parents, children, addresses, telephone numbers, medical details (especially if there are any special needs), and dates of birth. This way you can keep a track on birthdays and follow up parents who may be ill, having a baby or unable to attend for some reason. It also helps to keep the attendance numbers straight allowing newcomers in when there is room. Choose the right moment to ask for these details — not necessarily the minute they walk in the door but some time during the first visit if possible.

A welcome/information leaflet: Many groups design their own welcome/information leaflet. Here they make clear that the group is run by Christians and give all basic information necessary for a new member. They include such details as the starting and finishing times, cost, leaders' names, the structure of the session, toilet and nappy changing facilities, and the various play areas available — these are all important. These leaflets need to be positive and welcoming. Where there are guidelines on smoking, being responsible for one's own child and helping out with making the coffee and children's drinks, they need to be delicately and sensitively put so as to avoid a list of do's and don'ts! It can be a good idea to assign a leader to go through these details with newcomers and it also serves to establish a personal link. If they have come alone you can then introduce them to someone else in the group.

Newsletters: In addition to welcome/information leaflets, some groups produce regular newsletters which include details of church services, Sunday school or other groups suitable for young families in the church, such as pram services or discussion groups. Whatever you decide on, make it simple and remember that you may be producing it for a long time. Keep in mind those who do not read and others who prefer not to read. We live in an audio-visual age and so be sure to include as many pictures and illustrations as you can.

Such newsletters are easily produced with a photocopier and there are now numbers of magazines designed to assist in this process by providing titles, pictures, logos, and even appropriate jokes to create a more visual impact.

Initially it may seem hard work setting up your internal communications structure but once it is established it makes life a lot simpler. It can definitely be viewed as a long term investment of time.

On two occasions in the last ten years our own toddler group has actually closed down in order to reorganise its administration. This may sound drastic and it didn't go down too well with some of the parents but we felt it important enough to do so. New registration books were made and a more effective system created for accepting and welcoming new parents. In hindsight it was probably one of the best decisions we ever made!

1.13 Leadership

General aspects of leadership will be discussed in greater depth in a later chapter, but where parent and toddler groups are concerned the ratio of leaders to parents is critical if the work is to be effective. With strong administrative back-up our own group aims for three leaders to 25 parents on the register. In practice this rarely reaches more than 21 or 22 due to sickness, holidays, etc. Wherever possible we have at least one of those leaders with no children of their own so that they are free to handle a crisis and give undivided attention wherever it is required. One leader handles registration, another the daily activity leaving the third to 'float'. If we are all absorbed in a whirlwind of activity we cannot hope to build up any friendships.

Where there is a great demand for places at a group you may have to introduce a waiting list. It is far better to do this than be so overwhelmed by numbers that you lower standards and fail to achieve either long-term aims or short-term goals.

On my pinboard at home is a small CPO card advertising three different times for a parent and toddler group. It's there because it was, eight years ago, the fulfilment of my dream for that group. Today that church runs five sessions a week each of playgroup and toddlers as well as fortnightly pram services and discussion groups for enquirers. They now work alongside the health and social services and the church pay two part-time salaries for a co-ordinator and playleader. All this is because God 'is able to do immeasurably more than all we ask or imagine...' (Ephesians 3.20).

2
Christian Playgroups

Playgroups are not part of the statutory pre-school educational requirements but are legally registered voluntary groups set up by trained volunteers concerned for the development of children aged between two and a half and five years. Whilst parents play an important part in the running of groups they do not remain with their child during a playgroup session.

Before I became the mother of twins, I knew little about the stages of development of toddlers. But I soon found myself spending many hours trying to provide a variety of play experiences for my two. I saw here the value of constructive play. So when the church began to think about setting up a new playgroup I was glad to be involved. The parent and toddler group was bursting at the seams and few of the children's individual needs were being met.

We set out to convince the PCC of the need for a playgroup and then the practical necessities that accompany it like new toilet blocks, storage rooms, a 'wet' area and equipment, to name but a few! Hours were ploughed into prayer, plans and persuasion until finally we succeeded in convincing them on every account. Less than twelve months later the new buildings were completed, the playgroup registered, a playleader appointed, toys and equipment installed and a team of eager assistants trained and waiting for the arrival of the first of over forty children who had registered. I became one of those assistants and quickly realised that it was here and now that the work of lasting value began.

Penny was amongst the first of the new children. She was a small, pale, fragile-looking girl who clung tightly to her mother's skirt that first morning. Gradually though reluctantly over the next few weeks she allowed her mother to leave and spent time flitting from table to table, play area to play area, like a tiny lost sparrow. She was careful never to look anyone in the eye and rarely played 'with' anything or anyone. We prayed for Penny, loved and sought to assist her in her play. This was new territory for me and I watched this little girl's growth and development with fascination. It was an awesome responsibility and a tremendous privilege to be part of this child's life, and indeed the lives of all the children in that playgroup.

My time at playgroup was short-lived although I never lost contact with the leaders. I withdrew from the assistant's rota at the end of the first year. It was therefore a joy to be asked to attend the Rose Queen ceremony a year later and crown the queen. The well rehearsed procession made their grand entrance to the delight of the congregated parents, church members and local dignitaries. Following the speeches, the crowning ceremony and the taking of umpteen photographs we all settled ourselves for the entertainment. Among the action songs and singing rhymes came a solo spot. 'The Cuckoo Song' has never been sung in such a delightful and enchanting manner before or since. The singer? Penny. That tiny lost sparrow no longer existed. In its place was an outgoing, happy and purposeful child delighting in her new-found confidence. Penny had grown out of all recognition. It seemed like a miracle, the change was so marked.

If I had needed convincing of the value of playgroup work, that true story would have done it. Penny's parents were also drawn into the activity and life of the group and were thrilled with all they were to see and learn. The rippling effects of helping children at play are far-reaching, touching parents and siblings, as hundreds of playgroups have discovered over the years.

The playgroup movement began in the early 1960s through a generation of parents who could be described as 'post-war' parents. Their lives had probably witnessed more change than any others this century with increased opportunities and greater freedom than at any other time. During this time the Pre-School Playgroups Association (PPA) was formed to advance the education of children below compulsory school age. Today this body is one of the most influential voices in its field in the country. It has earned the respect and audience of the educational, social and health services. It produces many resources and books on vital subjects such as child development and playgroup organisation and activity. The PPA is without doubt the 'expert' ready and willing to guide those who wish to learn all that is necessary in playgroup work and I thoroughly recommend them.

My chief concern in what follows is to look at some of the issues and concerns facing those playgroups who would call themselves 'Christian'.

2.1 What makes a playgroup 'Christian'?
Hundreds of playgroups throughout the country meet on church premises. The large rambling buildings that lie vacant between Monday and Friday often lend themselves to playgroup activity. The majority of these church-based playgroups are run by parents in the community who simply pay for the use of the premises. Occasionally there might be an interest expressed by the church members or a representative on the playgroup committee, but generally speaking the two organisations work quite independently of each other.

There have been recent attempts in the form of publicity leaflets to make churches more aware of the under fives groups that use their premises. The introduction to one of these reads: 'Approximately 200,000 families come into playgroups... on church premises in England and Wales. Here is an open door to young families who may be outside your church. It is another way to step into your community.'

This is quite a challenge to those churches who keep a distance between themselves and the occupants of their buildings midweek.

There are however those who do not need reminding of both the privileges and opportunities presented to them through playgroup work. Many churches have taken the initiative in setting them up and see them as an integral part of the life and activity of the whole church. Here no distinction is made between the playgroup and any other Sunday or midweek group such as Sunday School, Boys' Brigade, etc. These 'Christian' playgroups (as opposed to 'church-based' playgroups who simply use church premises) are a conscious and deliberate attempt on the part of the church to serve and reach out into the community.

2.2 What are the priorities of a Christian playgroup

The stated aims of a Christian playgroup are not necessarily different from those of a secular group. They are essentially the development and growth of a child through play and the involvement of families and community in that important process. The difference lies more in the way in which we understand that development is part of an important on-going creative process that begins and ends in the hands of God. The psalmist reminds us of this in Psalm 139:

> You created every part of me;
> You put me together in my mother's womb...
> When my bones were being formed,
> Carefully put together in my mother's womb,
> When I was growing there in secret,
> You knew that I was there —
> You saw me before I was born.
> The days alloted to me
> had all been recorded in your book,
> before any of them ever began.

It is an awesome thing to realise that each individual child entering our playgroups has been 'put together' by God, and it is a tremendous privilege to be assistants to him in the developing process of their young lives. We also face the challenge of communicating something of this creator God to the parents and families of our children. Jesus often used children to illustrate important eternal truths to the adults of his day and we have the opportunity to use the same visual aid. I believe that God played an important part in the change in Penny over her two-year period in playgroup. He was as delighted as we were to see her progress. There were times when we were able to testify to God's part and communicate something of his nature and character. We can never force parents to see their child's development as part of God's restoring and developing work amongst his people, but as Christian leaders we have a vital part to play in it — especially where little ones are concerned.

The church foundation and strong Christian viewpoint held by Christian playgroups can mean a difference in structure and organisation from those of secular groups. It is some of these areas that I want to consider in this chapter.

2.3 Government and control of a Christian playgroup
It is in the area of the government and control of playgroup life that the Christian group differs most from the secular. The secular group strongly emphasises the principles of community involvement and parent committee control. The playgroup movement as a whole is committed to these principles and they form the basis of the recommendations made by PPA on playgroup management. The origins of this thinking lie in the conviction that parents have much both to give and gain in being involved with their child's development.

In order to protect the wider vision of a Christian playgroup many churches choose to place the overall control in the hands of their central church governing body, not the parents. This church body, whatever it might be, makes the major decisions affecting the organising structures. These decisions may include matters such as the appointment of the leaders, structure of the committee, fund-raising policy and the amount of Christian teaching to be included (if at all) within the playgroup. Churches will vary on what they consider to be the important decisions and in their opinions on these matters.

The practical day-to-day running of the group is usually delegated to the leaders and parents, i.e. those who have most to offer and benefit from being involved at this level.

Making known the structures
Whatever structures we adopt as Christian groups, it is very important that we make them known to the members who attend. Our parents who pay for a playgroup service have a right to know who is responsible and how the group is organised. If they have a part to play in those structures they need to understand exactly what is expected of them.

Most secular groups make their governing structure and powers known through a constitution which clearly outlines the aims and organisation of the group. A constitution is also required if a group wishes to apply for charitable status. Large numbers of secular playgroups adopt the constitution recommended by the PPA as it automatically gives them charitable status.

Christian playgroups can claim their charitable status from the church and therefore do not require a constitution for this particular purpose. This can and sometimes does lead to complacency about making known their governing and organisational structures. Some adopt the PPA constitution believing (wrongly so) that as a Christian group their church body has ultimate control! In fact, a strong conviction about parent participation and control is reflected in the PPA constitution. Other Christian groups simply don't do anything at all, leaving parents unaware of exactly who has the power to say or do anything in relation to the group.

Making the structures known is not a difficult task. An explanatory leaflet simply stating the foundation of the group, its aims, who carries responsibility for it and the organising committee structure, if it has one, is not difficult to produce.

Group and leader protection

Without some kind of written record of the aims, governing structures and organisations of our playgroups we can become extremely vulnerable. The sudden departure of church or playgroup leaders with whom the unrecorded vision and organisation of the group lies could result in the group's collapse or take-over by unqualified persons. We need to protect the aims and vision of our group.

Of equal importance is the protection of leaders within the playgroup, especially where leaders are employed for considerable numbers of hours. Job descriptions and terms of employment should be drawn up, and in some cases where the work is extensive actual statements may need to be signed as proof that both worker and employer have agreed to certain particulars. Do make sure that you know what National Insurance stamps ought to be paid. Details of the level at which these should be paid can be found at the contributions section of your local Department of Social Services.

Good organisation and recording of all these matters also help the continuity of a group in the inevitable turnover in leadership.

A live church link

Where central church government and control do exist in Christian groups, it is very important that this vital link is seen to be alive and working. On occasions Christian playgroup workers feel isolated and alone in their midweek activities. They need as much prayer, encouragement and support as any church group leader whether it be the Sunday School teacher or housegroup leader. Regular reports back to the church council or deaconate are very important, and this needs to be reciprocated by their attendance at some of the open activities such as fundraising events or open days. Some further suggestions of how to encourage church support are considered in chapter 6.12.

2.4 Leaders and assistants within a Christian playgroup

Whilst nearly all Christian groups appoint a committed church member as leaders in charge, many vary in their policy over the appointment of assistants or helpers within their playgroup. There are those who insist on all leaders being Christians, whilst others are quite happy to involve and include those who are not church-attenders. Many groups don't feel that they have the choice, the need outweighing the availability of church folk able and willing to offer their time.

There are arguments for and against on this issue. Where there is a high percentage of Christian helpers from the church the links and strength of vision for the work can be much stronger, but of equal importance is the involvement of parents. Many are helped and supported in their parenting through their involvement and others have much to offer in terms of time, energy and skills. We should never underestimate the value of working alongside parents both in what we have to share with them and in what we receive from them.

Relationships between leaders

The atmosphere within playgroups is so often determined by the relationships between the leaders and assistants. Healthy relationships are a tremendous source of strength but unhealthy ones can be destructive. Tensions and personality clashes affect the whole group and Christians are not exempt from such problems. The whole area of relationships in Christian groups is one which will come under fire from the enemy. We need to pray hard and work hard at our relationships and not allow negative and destructive attitudes to break down the good that God is doing in the group.

With this in mind many leaders try to pray together at the start of a session and in particular at planning meetings. In a Christian group God is the foundation stone on which it is built, and as leaders we need his help and strength in all that we do. Where prayer is introduced sensitively and meaningfully it need not cause discomfort or embarrassment to anyone. On the contrary, it serves to strengthen the bonds that exist between us as Christian leaders.

Leadership training
The leaders and assistants also determine the quality of the play environment in a playgroup. Training is of the utmost importance in this respect. I know from personal experience that academic qualifications or professional skills in other fields do not necessarily equip you for the job of play leading. Sadly there are some Christian groups who are reluctant to join in the excellent courses run by PPA and Social Services, perhaps considering themselves exempt from the need for training. As Christian groups we should always be prepared to learn as well as share our own experiences in training courses. We need at all times to set high standards. Other aspects of leadership training are covered in chapter 6.7.

2.5 Outreach and witness within a Christian playgroup

The extent to which a Christian playgroup should witness amongst parents and children is a question every group faces. Opinions differ from group to group. Much depends upon how we understand Christian witness and our approach to it.

There are some who seek actively to create as many opportunities as they can to share Christ both within the playgroup session and amongst the parents. This may include the teaching of Christian stories, singing of Christian songs, compulsory prayers as well as full acknowledgement of Christian festivals. There is a strong expectation that parents will support and join in many of these activities. Every opportunity is taken to involve them in discussion groups or invite them to church. For these groups a direct approach to their witness is a high priority.

Probably an equal number of groups view their witness differently. They feel that they have to earn the right to share their faith. Whilst the Christian foundation of the group is made very clear to parents and the church involvement is quite obvious, they prefer to demonstrate their faith through their actions rather than in words. The inclusion of Christian teaching within the session is occasional, presuming no right to impose their faith upon the children.

Where Christian groups are operating in multi-faith and multi-cultural areas the question of Christian outreach and witness is much more complex. In some of the most highly populated of these areas there are clear-cut regulations and guidelines set down by Social Services and local authorities. Some groups are obliged to inform Social Services of any Christian content to their playgroup session.

Having lived and worked for eleven years in one of the most densely populated Asian areas of Bradford, I know from first hand experience just how difficult it can be to face up to some of the issues that surface as a result of being in a multi-faith and multi-cultural community. It is hard to think things through from a Christian standpoint and a lot easier to bury our heads in the sand. There are many individual Christians and churches who refuse to even recognise their neighbours. Loving them regardless of colour, race or religion is a challenge to us all.

We can also carry around a great deal of racial prejudice unawares! I did so for a long time and so do urge any one who lives in multi-faith and multi-cultural areas to find somebody to assist you in your thinking and understanding of the problems that you will face.

In all our dealings with families and children we need to be *aware*, *honest* and *loving*, whatever their belief or chosen lifestyle. As Christians we spend a lot of time trying to achieve through our activity. Sometimes it is good to stop and check our attitudes and allow God to work through them.

Be aware. In order to understand our children and families, particularly those from other faiths and cultures, we need to understand the backgrounds from which they've come. We have a responsibility to find out about their family structures, major religious festivals and customs, the foods they can and cannot eat and the times at which the families are fasting. We need to show both parent and child that we are interested in them as people whatever lifestyles they practice. Our ignorance may well pull a small child in two and bring unbearable pressures.

There are an increasing number of Christian organisations now working amongst Asian communities in Britain whose workers are delighted to come and share with other Christian workers about the faith and culture of the people among whom they live and work. Much of the work at this level is done among the women and children who are at home during the day, and this is a particular source of help to those of us working in playgroups.

Be honest. This may be stating the obvious, but sadly it does need to be said. We need to make it very clear if we intend to speak about our faith within the playgroup sessions. Many parents will not show any concern at all, but others might and they have a right to know.

Interestingly we never did have any objections from Asian parents in Bradford as they rarely considered Christianity a serious threat to their religion and culture. Indeed, many were happy to allow their children to learn about other faiths and cultures and take part in Christian festival services. However there were occasionally parents of white children who did make inquiries as to exactly what was being said and done. At such times we had a responsibility to be totally honest with them.

I heard recently of a white British family who objected to their son playing the part of Joseph in the playgroup nativity on the grounds that their family had no wish to celebrate any Christian festival. Whatever our feelings about the beliefs of our parents, we must respect their wishes.

Be loving. Jesus' love for us is not dependent on who or what we are. His love is unconditional. It is this love that we need to show towards others whatever their colour, creed, or religion. One of my heroines is Mother Teresa of Calcutta. The love that this tiny Roman Catholic nun has for the poor and sick in India is incredible. She rarely needs words to communicate it — the love of God just shines through her. Oh that we as playleaders could demonstrate that powerful, compelling love to our parents and children.

Whatever we decide concerning the approach to outreach and witness within our groups, one thing we can all do is pray. Very often you hear Christians say, 'All we can do is pray,' implying that prayer is a pathetic last resort. Pray is not all, but *everything* that we can do. It is here that God will begin his work as we bring each child and parent before him, not only when there is a trauma or specific problem but regularly praying that they will grow and develop as whole people in body, mind and spirit. The work of the Holy Spirit in the lives of our families starts with our prayers for them. Some practical suggestions as to how we can pray together as leaders for our work can be found in a later chapter.

2.6 Care and concern within a Christian playgroup

We live in an age where care and concern within local communities appear to be decreasing. In the cities jobs are being created by local councils in order to pay people to care for the elderly, the lonely and the needy. There was a time when this type of visiting with encouragement and practical support was a natural and spontaneous part of community life.

The whole ethos of playgroups, Christian or not, is based upon care and concern. Their voluntary basis is an important factor. No one is in it for financial or personal gain. In caring for children and involving parents it is only natural that as leaders and assistants we become aware of their needs as we work alongside each other. A listening ear and the offer of advice or practical support are frequently a natural extension of playgroup life.

A large proportion of the children attending groups come from single parent families and are in particular need of support and encouragement. As well as offering our own concern there are a number of self-help groups we can put them in touch with. Some of these are listed in chapter 7.2.

We need to remember that the care we offer is not simply human compassion but an expression of God's love for these people. A friend told me recently of her time spent in a children's hospital working alongside the chaplain. All the staff in that hospital were deeply caring and compassionate people. Every one knew that. The role of the chaplain was not to compete with others in trying to show more concern but to offer an added dimension — that of God's concern and compassion in their time of need. Likewise as Christian playleaders we are called to offer that added dimension. Of course there will always be those who choose to reject it but our responsibility is to give it.

We regularly prayed for all our children and families but especially when any of them were ill. Where possible one of us would visit and offer to pray for them. Sometimes it felt appropriate to tell them that we were praying whilst on other occasions they would gladly welcome us to pray with them or with the child concerned. Many tears have been shed together over hospital beds and in some cases at funerals but they demonstrated the care and concern of a Father God. Words aren't always necessary at these times. Sometimes a card, book or simply just being there communicates God's love.

2.7 Relationships with outside agencies
One of the general criticisms made of playgroups is that they can be very inward-looking. Christian groups are probably more prone to this than secular groups. When the overall control is

from within the church there is a tendency to become self-sufficient and consequently reluctant to be part of the larger community and supporting agencies. So what positive links can a Christian group make?

The Social Services are probably the first outside agency that a playgroup comes into contact with because of the legal requirement of registration. It may take time to build up relationships with social workers but it is very important that we work together in the field of pre-school education. We should not allow negative thinking and destructive relationships to build up. As Christians and church bodies we need to earn the respect of these agencies.

The long term benefits of healthy relationships with social, health and educational services are tremendous. Many of the local health visitors and midwives would pop in to our group regularly — the clinic was conveniently placed opposite the church. The nurseries close by would attend the playgroup open days and take the opportunity to get to know the leaders. As time went on we were able to work together for the benefit of local families in need.

Students from local schools and colleges would also join us from time to time, some simply to observe the children at play whilst others had on long-term placements within the group. Even the probation service sought our help in the placing of young people on compulsory community service placements. All of these arrangements were the direct result of years of building up strong relationships with these outside agencies.

The value of joining the Pre-school Playgroups Association cannot be overstressed. Not only do you gain access to such things as training courses, bulk buy sessions and well thought out insurance coverage, but you also have the experience and advice of a national network of volunteer staff and a voice speaking on behalf of children and families to the government and other bodies. Christian groups have much to give and receive in getting involved in the work of PPA.

There are some very exciting projects going on in the field of pre-school education that have been initiated by Christians in local churches. Their growth and success have commanded the respect and support of many of the outside agencies working in this field. Playgroups have often been the starting point of these projects as the church began to recognise the needs of young families in their local community and seek to serve them in and through the work of their playgroups.

Playgroup life can be very absorbing. At times it may seem to dominate your entire life and no matter how many hours worked there is always more that can be done. The ideal, super-efficient, slickly organised, stimulating and challenging group sometimes feels a long way off. The reality is more likely to be long waiting lists, minimum funds, a shortage of leaders, untidy store cupboards and one or two uncontrollable hyperactive children, and the end of term gives just enough time to draw breath, see to your own family needs and start again.

There are times when you wonder if it is really all worth it. But occasionally I would walk to school to collect the children with the playleader from our last church. You could guarantee that every two or three paces she would stop and talk to a baby, mother or child. The conversation would range from how little Ben was getting on at nursery school to a developing pregnancy or sick mother-in-law! There was very little that she didn't know or have a concern for in almost every young family in the parish. I also knew that this concern was channelled into prayer. Their joys, needs and anxieties are God's concern.

It is impossible to evaluate a work of this kind. We can not quantify results and I know that most of us don't want to. We do however need to be encouraged and at these times it is good to sit back and picture in our minds the number of children, parents and indeed whole families whose lives have been influenced by our Christian playgroups. We should never underestimate the influence of God upon these families' lives. We may not see the fruit of these years of labour but God does and he knows the hard work and prayer that goes into our Christian playgroups.

Part Two
CHILDREN IN THE CHURCH

Introduction — Children and God

As both Christian parents and leaders of under fives groups we need to consider seriously where our children stand before God and consequently the importance of our church services to them. The understanding that we gain in doing this will not only affect the content of our services but give us a greater understanding of the role that we can play in nurturing their relationship with God.

Children are often described as the church of tomorrow. The implication made here is that they are just an appendage to the church until they reach adulthood. Jesus' teaching was quite different. He saw children as the church of the day.

There are many accounts in the Bible of Jesus being with children but the most well known is undoubtedly the occasion on which Jesus rebuked the disciples for turning children away. Mark's Gospel records it like this in chapter 10:

> People were bringing the children to Jesus to have him touch them, but the disciples rebuked them. When Jesus saw this he was indignant. He said to them, 'Let the little children come to me, and do not hinder them for the kingdom of God belongs to such as these. I tell you the truth, anyone who will not receive the kingdom of God like a little child will never enter it.' And he took the children in his arms, put his hands on them and blessed them.

What can we learn from this encounter? Three very important things stand out in this passage:
- Jesus hugged the children.

- Jesus included the children.
- Jesus took the children seriously.

Jesus hugged the children
'*Let the little children come to me.*' What better place than a service for bringing children to Jesus. Despite the disciples' attempts to keep them in the background, he makes it clear that they are loved and welcomed. We can presume that some were very young as he '*took the children in his arms*'. Whatever the age, sex, colour or size of a child they are important to Jesus. Making the way clear for children to come to Jesus is an important task — one that we should take very seriously.

In New Testament times young children would have had their faith nurtured in the home from birth. Jesus grew up in a family where prayer and worship centred around the family meal table. There children had a very important part to play and they would be expected to grow in their understanding and knowledge of God. Jesus' parents would have been the first to read scripture to him and later he would have attended the synagogue with his friends where they would be taught by the rabbis. As modern-day Christian families we have much to learn from the early Judeo-Christian tradition about living and growing in our faith together as families.

There is no doubt as to the value God places on children. The old Testament includes many accounts of children playing a vital role in the lives of God's people. Samuel was called as a young boy, both David and Joseph were but youths when they were spoken to by God and Naaman's servant girl played a vital part in his healing. Likewise there are many incidents recorded in the New Testament involving children. The healing of Jairus's daughter, the rejoicing of the children in the courts of the temple, the boy who offered Jesus his lunch in order to feed the great crowds, to mention but a few. There can be no doubt that God holds children very close to his heart. Isaiah 40.II says it like this: '*He tends his flock like a shepherd, he gathers the lambs in his arms and carries them close to his heart.*'

Jesus included the children

Three out of the four Gospel writers actually record this meeting between Jesus and the children and each of them includes the phrase *'for the kingdom of God belongs to such as these.'* There is no doubt or condition attached to this statement, it comes to us unqualified.

But didn't Jesus spend most of his time teaching and challenging the adults about this same kingdom? Yes. Does this mean then that the kingdom that we are being challenged with already belongs to the children? Seemingly, yes! Will they then always remain part of the kingdom of God? Not necessarily!

In his book *Children and God* Ron Buckland puts it like this: 'God views each child with favour and that... favour continues until the child turns his back on it...' (p.45).

With the right nurturing children may never actually turn their back on God, especially if their understanding and experience of him grows along with their social, physical, intellectual and emotional development. However that is not always the case. Many of us Christian parents know only too well the pain of watching our children reject all that we have faithfully tried to live out and teach. We are called to nurture our children in the faith but are not held totally responsible for their response to that as they alone stand accountable before God. Ron Buckland continues to say: 'As the child grows older he is in an increasingly dangerous situation because he is moving from total dependence on his parents towards direct accountability towards God.'

What does this say to us about the children who come into our church services from homes and families with little or no Christian influence? Basically that they are loved and accepted by God as part of his kingdom, and as leaders we have the awesome responsibility to nurture that relationship. The influence that we have upon them will allow the 'light' of the kingdom of God within them to kindle and shine as they grow. For many that influence will be short-lived, perhaps only a few months or possibly a few years. Many may never attend church again. It can feel like a hopeless task with seemingly little to show for our hard work. At such times we need to remember that we are privileged to be one of the first to speak about Jesus to these children. The impression we give of him will undoubtedly stay. First impressions are often lasting ones. So we need to be sure that we convey positive, happy, loving and safe messages about Jesus and his people.

As leaders we may be the ones who sow the very first seeds of spiritual awareness. We have the assurance of knowing that God is the sower of seeds, and those seeds remain in the hearts of people wherever they are or whatever they do with their lives. Their only experience of prayer might be the pram service prayer, their only experience of worship might be the family service choruses, their only knowledge of the Bible the stories told to them at a playgroup storytime. But in the years to come when they find themselves needing comfort, hope and love it will be these experiences that they will recall, these memories that will remain and these seeds that will begin to bear fruit in their lives.

It is amazing just what people will hold onto in their time of need and our efforts however fraught they might seem will not be wasted. As a clergyman my husband is continually meeting bereaved people, many of whom have not entered church since they were children. When it comes to choosing hymns and recalling prayers for their comfort it is those of Sunday school days that surface. It may seem a very small stone to build on but it is there and can be an important link in a chain when you are trying to bring comfort to these people and draw them closer to God.

We need to remember that through our services we also bring parents under the influence of the kingdom which gives added hope and encouragement for the nurturing of the child's faith. Ideally it is a ministry to the whole family — the touch of God upon both parent and child alike. The way we speak of Jesus will also influence the way parents will communicate to their children. They may well model themselves on our approach.

Jesus took children seriously
Children possess the qualities that adults need in order to enter the kingdom and therefore are an example to us.

> 'I tell you the truth, unless you change and become like little children you will never enter the kingdom of heaven.'
> 'Therefore whoever humbles himself like this child is the greatest in the kingdom of heaven.'

Jesus actually used the children as visual aids to challenge the adults with the message of God's kingdom. We may well ask, exactly who is leading who? Here in our children are the spiritual qualities that God looks for in us. Too often as adults we want to see outward signs as evidence of spirituality. We judge a person's spirituality by what they can express verbally, how they worship or even by their usefulness to the church. It is some years before a child can say, 'I want to follow Jesus,' or read the liturgy and hymns correctly, and even longer before they can give generously or serve on an important committee! And yet we are told, 'Unless you become as children you will never enter the kingdom of heaven.' Children are vulnerable, often helpless beings, dependent upon others for their existence. Above all else they are humble and surely these qualities of utter dependence and humility are the ones that God so desires to see in our own adult lives. As God's children we need to realise our helplessness before him and our inability to save ourselves. As children we must come...

There have been times when my own children have taught me more about the kingdom than any book or sermon. Some years ago Blue Peter were appealing for T-shirts for the Third World. My daughter, then four, went upstairs and turned out her drawers, 'Send these, mummy,' she said. 'They are too small for me. And these two as well.'

I pointed out that the latter two that she handed to me were in fact two of her newer T-shirts, 'I know,' came the reply, 'but I have four T-shirts and those children have none — it's best that we have the same and then it's fair.'

Perhaps if we did have a few children on our church committees the church both here and in the Third World would be in a healthier state!

The task that we face both as parents and leaders of services may feel daunting at times but the privileges are many. We soon come to realise that the learning is shared, a two way process between children and adults as we offer each other all that God has given to us.

3
Pram Services

Pram services are informal midweek services that aim to introduce pre-schoolers and their parents to the Christian faith and worship.

An elderly lady talking in a local post office one day was heard to say to a friend, 'Have you heard what the church is doing now? Once a month on a Tuesday at two o'clock you can get your pram repaired! Whatever next will they think of!'

That parish's well advertised pram services had been somewhat misinterpreted! In fact such services see few prams but plenty of buggies and baby-slings. Some groups have tried to incorporate 'buggy' into the title — with limited success. There are clearly problems when it comes to naming them. Some groups prefer a completely different approach such as 'Praise Parties' or 'Little Angels' whilst others simply describe the event as 'Under fives worship' or 'Children's Services'. The latter may imply that adults are not welcome which in most cases couldn't be further from the truth.

Whatever the name there is no doubt that these times of informal worship for adults and children are increasing in popularity. They seek to provide in a variety of different ways a half hour or more of singing, praying, storytelling and activity in the presence of God.

3.1 Why run a pram service?
Pram services are ideal stepping stones between church and community. They can incorporate something of a Sunday on a midweek day. Many families simply couldn't cope with the

culture shock of attending a Sunday family service. The unfamiliar surroundings, books, language, and even appearance of the clergy in dog collars are great hurdles to those who have never stepped inside a church before.

A pram service which is led by familiar people, perhaps the playgroup leader, and held in familiar surroundings like the church hall, will go a long way towards making people feel relaxed and receptive before God. They are also an opportunity to offer without apology something specifically Christian. Many parent and toddler groups and playgroups do not include any direct Christian teaching in their programmes but take full advantage of the friendships formed in these groups in inviting them to a pram service.

Pram services are also a means of bringing the children to Jesus, taking seriously that command from our Lord. There will be many children for whom a pram service will be their only experience of Jesus and Christian worship. We need to pray that it will be a lasting experience.

3.2 When to run a pram service

Think carefully about the best time to run a pram service. Many churches incorporate them into their playgroup or toddler programmes just two or three times a year at major festivals, i.e. Christmas, Easter and Harvest — usually at the beginning or end of a term. Others hold them regularly as an event in their own right either monthly, fortnightly or weekly. The frequency will depend on a number of practical factors like facilities, resources and leadership but, as is always the case in under fives work, it is better to start with something small and build up than aim too high and miss out completely. If they are just once a month it is a good idea to produce a card or leaflet with the dates on to remind parents.

In selecting a time do check with other under fives groups that may run in your area so as not to clash with them. Depending on the age group of the majority of the children, try to avoid 'sleep time'. Mornings are often busy times for parents, and if you run your services in the afternoons make sure that you finish in plenty of time for collecting older children from school.

3.3 Where to run a pram service

Enormous thick pillars, long narrow aisles and high hard pews are not always the best environment in which to sit comfortably with under fives for a pram service — especially if the church heating is inadequate which most systems are. Under these circumstances it is probably better to go into a church hall or lounge where you can sit informally with children on rugs or blankets with parents seated around them in a 'U' shape rather than in straight rows.

There are, however, advantages in meeting in the actual church building itself if the right environment can be created. Perhaps a certain section of the church can be rearranged to form a children's corner or chairs positioned informally in the chancel area with the children seated on the floor. Actually getting parents across the threshold of the church door and familiarising themselves with the furniture and fabric, however foreign it might be, is very important in preparation for the day they may want to attend on a Sunday and its value should not be underestimated.

One particular Christmas pram service in Bradford remains vivid in my memory for this very reason. Taking part in this dramatic production of the nativity were no less than thirty angels, tens of shepherds and far more than three wise men. (We did stick to the one Mary and Joseph although poor baby Jesus became the object of a 'tug-of-war' half way through.) On that occasion the church was packed to the doors with between 200 and 250 parents, grandparents, aunts, uncles and what felt like half the population of Bradford. (My husband's appearances at pram services as the vicar were few and far between but on this occasion I challenged him to come along and name ten of the folk present. He couldn't and had to confess that the church had never been so full of 'outsiders' before.)

As I was leading the service, at one particular stage I invited the congregation to take photographs. What followed is hard to describe but I think the closest comparison would be a stampede of journalists charging for the hottest news item of the year! Initially I was speechless (and that takes some doing) and quite horrified that so many 'outsiders' were taking over 'our' church service... until it hit me that they saw it as their church service in which they felt completely at home and free to act and behave naturally. They were not rigid, uncomfortable and silent as we so often see at baptisms. weddings and funerals where 'outsiders' come in reluctantly and out of obligation rather than choice.

Admittedly it took some minutes to restore order so that the service could continue on its planned course, but it was a welcome deviation on that occasion which helped us to realise the true value of bringing people into the church building.

3.4 Who should run a pram service?

Having already admitted that my own vicar husband runs a mile at the thought of leading thirty two- and three-year-olds in twenty minutes of holy chaos, I must admit that he is not alone. Ministers who have 'know-how' to make it their speciality and to become involved with pram services are few and far between. Some however do exist! More are likely to want to help initiate them in their churches. On the whole, ask for support and encouragement from your clergy and ministers along with the occasional attendance at a service to demonstrate their concern and at least show the parents that they do exist in person.

In my mind there are three essential qualities necessary for a leader of pram services: prayer, commitment, and a willingness to learn! Obviously an understanding of and desire to be with under fives is important, but contrary to what many think you do not necessarily have to be a teacher, nursery nurse or trained and skilled in any specific way. Some of our finest leaders over the years have been those who have learnt 'on the job'.

Preparing and planning a pram service is not something that can be done the night before but requires the sort of thought and care that is best given by two or three people. Having many different parts such a service lends itself to several people helping out, for example with singing, prayers, storytelling, activity time, and therefore team work with an overall leader becomes a natural way of working. The services themselves can be quite exhausting, not to mention the preparation and clearing up at the end!

3.5 How do under fives learn?
Children may be small people but they are not little adults. We need to understand and consider the way in which under fives learn and develop before planning our pram services. We need to take into account the physical, intellectual, social and emotional needs of under fives and this will influence the content of the service. Of course there is a wide range of development within the nought-to-five age group itself and we need to plan with those differing stages in mind, remembering of course that immobile children will more than likely be supervised by a parent.

At certain times in your pram service year you may have a majority of younger or older children and therefore have to adapt accordingly. Flexibility is the key at all times. We can apply a few general guidelines to the whole age range though, and it might help if we see them in terms of what under fives *don't* and *do* need within a pram service programme.

They *don't* concentrate for long. The guide is one minute for every year of development. Little wonder they won't listen to a ten-minute story! So keep each item to three or four minutes maximum.

They *don't* think abstractly. Most of our spiritual terms are abstract. So, for example, 'Jesus lives in our heart' or 'Jesus went to live with his father in heaven' is most likely to be responded to by an under five with 'Does Jesus get messed up with my tea when he's in my heart?' and 'Did Jesus get to heaven in an aeroplane or can he fly like superman?' Whilst Christian families have plenty of opportunities to answer such questions, a pram service child may not have that help.

They *don't* learn by listening, reading or writing!

They *don't* like the unfamiliar, so don't expect too much of the new child especially when it comes to joining in noisy and boisterous items. Be sensitive to the clingy child and make him or her feel welcome even if sitting on mum's knee.

They *do* need to *move*! — at least every two to three minutes. If you don't build movement into your service, they will! The results may not be all that you desire. Singing, dancing, actions and sounds all give opportunity for movement — an essential requirement.

They *do* need to *experience* for themselves. Any playleader will tell you that under fives learn through what they experience — what they touch, feel, smell, taste, hear. We need to create as many of these learning experiences within the pram service as we can.

They *do* need to be *involved* in all that you are doing. Never underestimate the number of illustrations and activities required for the under fives. Objects, pictures, photographs, puppets, even flowers and animals all serve as excellent aids to involvement.

They *do* need to be able to *relate* to the stories you tell them. We need to find a point of contact with them in their world. 'Long ago' to them means yesterday and even 'before Granny was born' is too much for them to grasp. It may be as simple as, 'Have you got a dress/jumper with lots of different colours in?'

as you introduce the story of Joseph, or 'Has your mummy ever lost something?' as the start to the story of the lost coin.

3.6 Four elements to a pram service

The content of a pram service can be varied but items will generally fall into one of four categories: storytelling, singing, prayers, or creative activity. At the end of this chapter you will find a full list of resources to assist you in planning these various elements, including books suggesting themes and outlines for a service, tapes to assist you in leading singing, visual aids, ideas for craft activities, and the names and addresses of supportive groups and organisations that will supply you with on-going help and resources. Of course most of these cost money and your funds may be limited. There is little doubt that resources of this kind can save you hours of thinking and planning and can therefore be considered a great investment in the long term. On the following pages are a few simple points to assist you in your planning of each of these sections, stimulate your thinking and give you some ideas to get started.

Guidelines for Storytelling

Make sure that everyone is sitting comfortably and that you can have eye contact with all the children. This is absolutely essential — do avoid the pillars!

Aim to get across one simple point rather than a vast amount of detail.

'Tell' a story, rather than read it, varying the tone of your voice and speed of speech, and repeat key phrases or words. Make use of the many excellent children's Bible stories available. Those written by Butterworth and Inkpen are creative and imaginative and will help you to tell a good story.

Encourage the children to join in with sound effects, e.g. 'clip clop' went the donkey, or 'Where are you little sheep?' said the shepherd looking for his lost sheep. Welcome their comments and contributions at all times. Don't be afraid to *ad lib*, when it comes to Bible stories. Use your imagination and recreate the scene in everyone's minds including the feelings of the characters, the reactions of others, the weather and the smells around them (those smelly fish!). Make the people and the situations come alive.

Keep the story short, no more than six to eight minutes at the most, including good visual aids.

Always illustrate what you are saying with objects, pictures, puppets, and anything else that you can find.

Guidelines for Singing

Keep the songs simple with no more than one syllable to a beat and mostly 2/4 or 4/4 time.

Use songs with repetition of words and build up a repertoire of favourites, without introducing too many new ones at once.

Involve the children in actions, if necessary making up your own.

Write your own words to familiar and traditional tunes like 'Three Blind Mice', 'Here we go round the mulberry bush' and 'Frere Jacques'. This is much easier than you might think and can be good fun.

Make use of the increasing numbers of children's worship tapes, especially if you find it difficult to sing or accompany singing time.

Provide musical instruments for the children — home-made rattles, drums, clappers, shakers, bells and triangles.

If you are musical try writing your own songs and choruses.

Encourage parent participation, especially when teaching new songs. You could even consider sending them home with copies of the words so that they can practise.

If you are artistic, consider illustrating simple songs with large colourful pictures. 'If I were a butterfly' and many others lend themselves to this perfectly and it serves to help the children remember the words.

Guidelines for Praying

Prayer needs to be a very natural part of our pram service and not simply the time when we close our eyes and put our hands together. Try to create an atmosphere in which we talk naturally to Jesus, sometimes quietly, other times noisily, alone or together.

Opening prayers can be noisy and bouncy times, e.g. all join hands together and shout 'Thank you God for pram service, hurray!'

Closing prayers may be quieter prayers as we say to each other 'God be with each of us here and in our homes. Amen.'

At some point in the service help the children to think of what they might say 'sorry', 'thank you' and 'please' for in their prayers. Make a prayer board with these three points on and use it to illustrate your prayers.

Try to link the prayers in with the theme of the pram service. As with the story time, objects can help focus the children's attention for prayer.

You may like to write your own pram service prayer that you say at each service with the children repeating each line after the leader.

Encourage response lines to follow each prayer, e.g. 'We are sorry, Lord Jesus' or 'Be with them, Lord Jesus'.

Make the prayers real to them and their lives. Pray for their families, especially when a new baby is due or someone is ill. Be prepared for the inevitable 'My grandad has died' or 'My daddy has left us'. These occasions require sensitive handling.

Prayer board

board made from a large cardboard box, unfolded and painted or covered

pictures stuck on with blu tack – changed each time

Puppets

wool

paper bag or fabric

wooden spoon

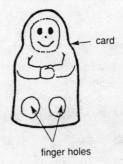

card

finger holes

'spoon' puppets and 'finger' puppets are two of the easiest to make

Activities:

Badge

write child's name here

Flag

a drinking straw

Sheep collage

stick on cotton wool

write child's name here

Guidelines for Activities

Keep in mind the limitations of the under fives in terms of their ability to cut, colour, glue, etc. Keep it simple. Sticking pre-cut shapes of gummed paper onto outlines is one of the easiest forms of activity for very small children.

Involve the parents at activity time.

Relate the activity in some way to the story.

Try making a group collage to which they can all contribute, e.g. cotton wool sheep with each of their names on placed onto a large background of a field.

Allow them to take home some things, e.g. badges, flags, hats, finger puppets, suggesting they put them in their bedrooms.

Have some toys available for younger children to play with.

3.7 Structuring a pram service

The exact order of your pram service is up to you but I'd like to suggest two sample outlines that you might find helpful in your planning. They are simply suggestions based on an approximate timing of one hour. Your own circumstances may be completely different. The detailed timing of these outlines are given not to imply a strict timekeeping but more to show how quickly you can get through prepared material. In practice you will discover that what may have taken days and weeks to prepare gets used up in minutes! It is rare to be able to stick rigidly to a precise timetable but it is a good discipline to plan with one in mind, and it gives you a secure base to work from.

Pram Service Outline — Example 1

1.50–2.00	Informal singing whilst everyone arrives.
2.00–2.02	Ring the pram service bell to indicate the start of the service.
2.02–2.05	One song to begin with, linked with the theme.
2.05–2.13	Story time using puppets.
2.13–2.15	Pram service prayer.
2.15–2.30	Activity time (all prepared in advance).
2.30–2.40	Song and chorus time including actions and dancing.
2.40–2.45	Prayer board time.
2.45–3.00	Refreshments.
3.00–?	Clearing up time and collapse!

Pram Service Outline — Example 2

1.50–2.00	Informal play with prearranged toys (which may be linked to the theme, e.g. dressing up clothes) whilst everyone is arriving.
2.00–2.04	Lighting of the pram service candle and saying together of the opening prayer.
2.04–2.10	Song and chorus time with musical instruments.
2.10–2.15	Prayer board time.
2.15–2.17	One chorus linked to the theme.
2.17–2.25	Story time.
2.25–2.30	Final song and prayer.
2.30–2.45	Activity time.
2.45–3.00	Refreshments.
3.00–?	Clearing up time and collapse!

3.8 Leading a pram service

The overall leadership of the pram service is important to ensure good continuity especially where there are several people taking part. Both children and parents need to know who is in control. If there are a few of you it may help to produce a service rota indicating who is doing which part.

The start and finish of a pram service are important times and it may help if some kind of ritual is introduced here. Children love the familiar, and a set routine in which they feel secure, such as the ringing of a bell or the lighting of a candle, are helpful. Opening and closing prayers also help at these times.

3.9 A Sample Pram Service

Here is a suggestion for a pram service based on the theme of Jesus as Healer.

Theme: Jesus the Healer.

Story: Jairus's Daughter. (In preparation read Matthew 9.8–18.) For ideas on how to begin and develop the story see 'Story development' below.

Useful books: *Becky Gets Better* (Palm Tree Press) or their Children's Bible (N.T.).

Visual Aids: For the story: glove puppets (girl, father, mother, Jesus, servants). Either make your own or purchase Celebration Screenprint puppet kits. A show box for the bed or a small child's cot with bedding. For the prayers: cut-out pictures or photographs of nurses, doctors, hospitals, sick children. The Jesus glove puppet.

Activity: A two-sided card cut-out of a girl, showing her on one side ill in bed and on the other side standing up and well. (see below.)

Songs: 'Jesus loves the little children
All the children of the world
Red and yellow, black and white

All are precious in his sight
Jesus loves the little children of the world.'
(Tune: Traditional)

'My God is so BIG.' (Music and words on 'Sing to
the King' cassette tape.)

Prayers: Using a prayer board as illustrated below, talk about all
the different people who help us when we are ill. Stick
appropriate pictures on the board to illustrate all you say.
Prepare no more than three or four simple sentences for prayer
based on your discussions, e.g. 'Thank-you, God, for our
mummies, daddies, doctors and nurses who look after us when
we are ill', 'Thank-you for Jesus who makes people better', 'We
are sorry for sometimes hurting our friends', 'Please make
well... (include names of friends and parents). Encourage the
children to join in a loud *Amen*!

Story development:
1. Begin with a game: 'Ring a ring of roses' or a shortened
   version of 'The Farmer's in his den'. (If the group has very
   young children and babies get them to play 'Round and
   round the garden like a teddy bear'.)
2. Introduce the little girl Becky as someone who loved to play
   these games but can't play them because she is ill.
3. Continue the story as developed in PTP book or Bible using
   the puppets, cot or box and bedding.
4. Allow the children to join in with musical instruments as the
   official mourners.
5. Finish the story and end by singing 'My God is so big'.

Activity instructions: You will need:
   pink card
   coloured sugar paper or coloured sticky back squares
   wallpaper or gift wrapping paper for bedclothes
   PVA glue and glue spreaders
   pencils and black crayons

  Advance preparations:
1. Make a card template of shape A (Becky) and shape B

(bedcover and stand), bedclothes (same as shape B), dress, coat, and hair.

2. For each person cut out in pink card, shape A and shape B.
3. Fold shape B along dotted line and stick the fold onto shape A at the line marked. (The bedcover will now fold up and down. When folded down it becomes the support for Becky to stand up.)
4. Cut out the bedclothes in pretty wallpaper or wrapping paper.
5. Cut out dress, coat and hair from sugar paper or sticky paper — shapes C, D and E. Use appropriate colours.

On the day preparations: Put out for each child/mum: cut outs A and B (already stuck together), and one set of bedclothes, hair, dress, coat.

Instructions to parents:
1. With girl in bed position, stick on bedclothes and draw in a sad face.
2. Pull back bedcovers and make stand. Turn girl round to other side.
3. Stick on dress, hair and coat.
4. Finally draw on a happy face.

I cannot end this chapter on Pram Services without sharing with you one of the bleakest and most difficult times that the team in our last parish ever experienced, yet from which some of the most important lessons were learnt.

We had given considerable prayer to the question of whether we should join in the church's annual children's mission in the local park. Normally the age range for this was from five years upwards. After much debate and prayerful conviction we decided to include the under fives. We began planning for five consecutive day services to be held in the open air for one hour each morning. The site was carefully selected and many hours preparation went into prayer and acquiring banners, polythene ground covering, blankets, deckchairs (for pregnant mums), flasks for coffee, umbrellas and so on, as well as all the normal

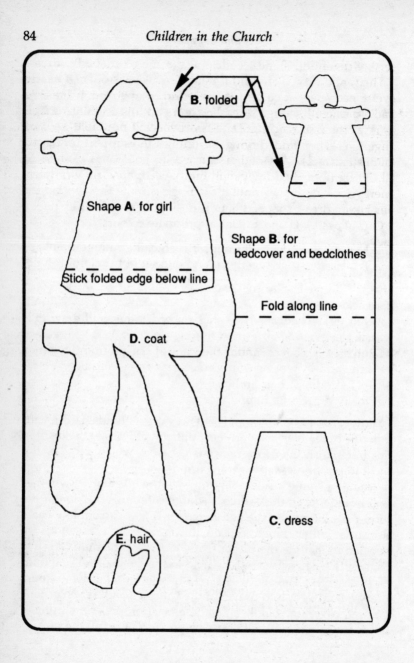

B. folded

Shape A. for girl

Stick folded edge below line

Shape B. for
bedcover and bedclothes

Fold along line

D. coat

C. dress

E. hair

service planning.

The week arrived and did it rain! The heavens opened nearly every morning — one day we were forced to abandon site. We had a particularly large team of leaders on this occasion as well as our fifteen or so children. They, believe it or not, were little angels, soaking up everying including the rain! A few of our faithful pram service mothers turned up but no newcomers at all. There was seemingly nothing to show for all that time, energy, prayer and planning. Some of us had even rearranged our holidays to be there.

Our dampened clothes and spirits caused us to ask the inevitable question: 'Why?' Didn't God know that we were already exhausted from the summer term? Did he realise the extra effort, energy and personal cost that each of us had freely given? Had we not listened carefully enough at the outset? Was it all so wrong and badly planned? Had not the whole church covered us in prayer — the weather being the top of the list? It was all too much to bear and I for one wasn't sure if I could face an autumn programme after this.

At the end of that week my Bible reading was as follows:

As the rain and the snow come down from heaven
and do not return to it without watering the earth,
and making it bud and flourish, so that it yields seed for
    the sower
and bread for the eater,
So is my word that goes out from my mouth;
It will not return to me empty
but accomplish that which I desire
and achieve the purpose for which I sent it.

I'm convinced that God has a sense of humour and I still smile when I read 'as the rain and snow'. Perhaps a small part of me is thankful that we only had rain!

I was so geared to looking for the 'outward' signs of success — large numbers, new parents, orderly services and long, deep and meaningful conversations afterwards. Instead it had been our own children, a few faithful mums and a quick dash through the services in order to take cover from the rain. We were doing our best and God was accomplishing his purpose. We had to learn to trust him, believing that indeed the word that we had proclaimed to however few or young in years would bear fruit in God's time.

Your pram services may never have hundreds in attendance, they may not be regular or frequent. But they are unique in God's eyes as they bring together parents and children in his presence. We make this special meeting possible and that delights our Father's heart.

4

Under Fives
on Sundays

This chapter identifies and discusses some of the difficulties encountered by under fives in Sunday services of worship. Practical suggestions are offered as positive means of welcoming, involving and including young children as part of the worshipping body of Christ.

Some years ago we as a family were privileged to spend several months in the United States of America working in the Epispocal Church in south-west Virginia. At the time of departure our twins were just seven and a half months old. We left behind us two sets of grieving grandparents struggling to come to terms with being separated from their new baby grandchildren for almost four months. I promised faithfully to write and report in detail on the number of teeth cut and movements made and to send photographs.

Over the weeks and months to follow I found the exercise of detailed progress reports both tedious and boring, especially as between them they had only produced one tooth! In an attempt to make the procedure more interesting I decided to write the letters as if I were the twins themselves. I tried to imagine how I would feel in their position being dragged all around the state of Virginia sleeping in different cots and homes almost every week, not to mention eating different foods and generally experiencing a difficult culture. (We may speak the same language as Americans but there the similarities end.) The results proved not only entertaining to the grandparents but a valuable exercise for me in understanding my children. It was the start of something I continue to do as they grow up, that is, to look at life through the eyes of a child.

This story inevitably leads up to the question, 'How do our under fives see the church on a Sunday?' I suspect that if a toddling two year old were able to write to their grandparents concerning their first visit to church it might read a little like this:

Dear Grandma,

This morning Mummy took me to church for the very first time. I thought we were going to Rainbow Toddlers because we went through the big giant's door but we weren't because the room was different and much bigger. It was cold, with nothing on the floor and we didn't take our coats off all the time we were there.

There was a man at the door who didn't know Mummy but he sort of smiled at her. She got a book and a piece of paper. I don't think he saw me because I didn't get anything, only the grown-ups did.

Auntie Joan was there from toddlers and my special friend Lucy. Lucy wasn't allowed to sit by me because she was with her Daddy and big sister. Our Daddy didn't want to come. I stood up on the seat to wave to Lucy but her Daddy told her to sit down and be good. I only wanted to wave. The lady behind us asked Mummy to take me off the seat because I was making it dirty so she carried me. I wanted to see the man who was talking.

Soon we started to play games. First it was dressing up but only the men at the front were allowed to play. It wasn't fair really because I wanted to put on a big dress like them. We all played hide-and-seek though, grandma, even the grown-ups. You get down and hide behind the seat, and when the man says the magic word 'Amen' you jump up again. They played that three times!

Singing time was good fun but I didn't know all the songs. They sang some that we sing in Rainbow Toddlers, clapping and dancing songs. There was a big space for dancing and jumping right between the seats but nobody used it. It was hard to dance in Mummy's arms but I made a big noise clapping. Lucy did too but her Daddy told her to be quiet. Grandma, can you clap quietly? The grown-ups were very good at it in church.

You have to pay to go to church, grandma. Two men came round with big big plates and collected all your money. Some people didn't have any money so they gave them an envelope instead. But you know something, Grandma, you didn't get any drinks and biscuits after you'd paid. They just gave it all to the man at the front. I think that he must be very rich.

Later the man at the front said that all the children had to go out, I think he was fed up of us. Mummy took me to the room where we have Rainbow Toddlers but it wasn't the same. Mummy wanted to go back into church to listen to the man talk about Jesus. Poor mummy — I'm sure it would be nicer for her to read my book about him. I played with Lucy for a while but then I wanted mummy to come back. The lady said that she wouldn't be long, but she was. I cried because I missed my mummy but Lucy kissed me better.

At the end, the man dressed up was standing by the door. He asked mummy if she had been before and said he hoped that she would come again. He shook mummy's hand. He didn't speak to me, I don't think he wants me to come again. Perhaps it's because I can't clap quietly or because I wanted to wave to Lucy. I didn't mean to dirty the seat, grandma — I only wanted to see.

I slept all afternoon when we got home. Daddy said I can go every week if it makes me sleepy, but grandma, I'm not sure if I want to go again.

Lots of love, Jannie xxxx

The psalmist said, 'I rejoiced with those who said to me, Let us go to the house of the Lord.'

How many of our under-fives rejoice at the thought of going

to the Lord's house? Or do they feel like young Jannie, 'I'm not sure if I want to go again'? As these little ones cross the threshold of that 'big giant's door', what are we saying to them both verbally and non-verbally?

Children of all ages have an innate ability to understand our messages even when they are subconsciously given. 'You're a nuisance' or 'Don't disrupt our service' or even 'We need you as adults so we'll put up with you now' comes through loud and clear. You can't fool children.

The introductory sentence to the service of Baptism of Children in the Anglican Service Book says this, 'Children who are too young to profess the Christian faith are baptised on the understanding that they are brought up as Christians in the family of the church.' It sometimes feels as if the church spends a lot of its time trying to keep the children out, not bringing them up 'within'. The report 'Children in the Way' published in 1988 highlights these very issues.

4.1 What kind of welcome do we offer?

The part of the service of baptism that I love the most comes towards the end. The congregation stand to welcome the baby into the church family using the following words:

> We welcome you into the Lord's family
> We are members together of the body of Christ
> We are children of the same Heavenly Father
> We are inheritors together of the Kingdom of God
> We welcome you.

Similarly in services of dedication of a child before God, prayers and statements of commitment are spoken by the church body as they accept their responsibility for the nurturing of the child's faith within the community of believers.

This is the time when the whole congregation focuses in thought and prayer on that one child. But it is also the part at which I ask myself, 'Can we as a body fulfil this awesome and privileged responsibility?' What sort of welcome do we offer these babies both now and in the future?

We are quick to criticise the parents for whom baptism or dedication is treated simply as a social custom or one of the innoculations administered for their future safety just like whooping cough jab. But are we so quick as a church to accept our responsibility in the process of Christian nurture? Whatever our denomination, do young parents and babies flock through our doors each Sunday morning drawn by our warm welcome and concern for the spiritual development of their children? Surely that welcome must begin at birth, from the very first time that a child enters church however small or young, whether for baptism, dedication or simply as a visitor.

Babies and small children are 'dependent' members of the body of Christ, just as old, sick or disabled members of our congregation are too. There will always be such dependent members of the body and therefore always a need for the body to accept a responsibility towards this group of people. It doesn't mean that they cannot contribute or that they have nothing to offer, but simply that they are dependent upon the body in order for their contribution to be of value or use.

It is often the housebound and disabled who pray most and they often offer great wisdom and insight on situations. Unless the body makes the effort to include them and receive them, they may remain unused as well as unseen and unappreciated.

Likewise children teach us many of the realities and truths of the Kingdom of God — they are living examples of dependency and trust, with a quickness to forgive, and so on, traits which Jesus so clearly commended. Without the contribution of these members we are in danger of missing out and being an incomplete body. We are *one* body called to serve one another, and in so doing we will learn about the grace and knowledge of our God.

Our view of children within the body cannot simply remain an attitude of heart and mind. It needs to be translated into a language and practice that children can both receive and absorb.

4.2 Under fives in worship

When the community of the church comes together to worship it comes as one body before God. The members of that body are many and varied, each with their different interests and levels of understanding. It is our task to discover a way in which the whole church can participate as one in worship.

Too often churches attempt to meet one particular interest group in worship, perhaps the elderly or the teens. Some go to the lengths of providing different and separate services in order to achieve this goal. Others change the emphasis week by week in order to keep everyone happy. In such cases the group of people whose interests are not considered for that week either become 'observers' or simply don't attend. This can only serve in the end to polarise our congregations and do little for the unity that we seek to achieve as the body of Christ.

There are many advocators of 'all-age worship' when literally all age groups come together to praise and sing, receive instruction, pray and learn actively together. Neither is there any pretence in the matter that introducing such worship involves thorough rethinking and total commitment from the church leadership. The motivation, time and energy involved are great but the benefits undoubtedly enriching for all concerned. In order to involve every age group there is no need to dilute the message to the lowest common denominator. Children, as we have said so many times, learn chiefly through what they experience and therefore will retain many varied experiences through active corporate worship of this kind. In her book *All-Age Worship* Maggie Durran discusses thoroughly the benefits of all-age worship as well as providing many suitable and varied scripts, readings, songs and ideas.

Many congregations choose to operate on a 'whole church family' service basis, children of all ages remain in the first half of the service after which they leave to receive instruction in the various age groups. Some follow the same teaching programme at every level including the adult sermon teaching time so that all members of the body are learning the same lesson at their own level.

Some congregations oppose the inclusion of small children in worship. In this case, however well motivated we may be to develop all-age participation or every level instruction programmes it is probably something beyond our immediate influence or control. Under these circumstances we need to work hard at the long-term problem of educating the congregation as well as seek to find ways and means of making Sunday worship a positive and valuable experience for our under fives. There are a number of practical things that can be done in order to give the under fives a sense of inclusion and involvement in our worship whatever it may be like.

4.3 Practical aids to worship

Under fives need to *see*. Hard pews and large pillars are hard to avoid in some of our churches. Small chairs at the end of pews or in front of the first pew can help. Alternatively floor cushions strategically placed or booster seats in the pews designed specifically for that purpose go a long way towards helping a toddler to see.

Secondly, under fives need to *move*. Yes, little pattering feet on stone floors can be a distraction to the silent prayers but less so if a small area of the church is carpeted allowing them that freedom to jump about. Carpet is also a lot safer for the inevitable tumbles of the toddler. It creates a far more homely atmosphere overall. Alternatively keep a supply of soft slippers nearby or encourage parents to bring their children's own slippers.

Putting these two points together might suggest a carpeted area at the front of the church where they can feel very involved.

Thirdly, under fives need to *exit*. Many crying babies remain in church because their parents don't know if they are allowed to go out or, if so, exactly where. A simple announcement or a small notice positioned where it can be read can alleviate a lot of tension in new and visiting parents. A billboard at the entrance or information on the service sheet are other common solutions. These also serve to prepare the rest of the congregation for movement that may well occur.

4.4 Aids to involvement and inclusion in worship

Singing: Hymn books are usually an integral aid to worship but are rarely given to a child under five years of age. True, they won't be able to read the majority of hymns, but is that a valid reason for making them feel excluded from this aspect of worship? Some may well try to chew the cover or drop them several times during the service, but how long do we wait before we consider them old enough to try and take part? It gives many a child a sense of belonging and welcome to be given books like all the grown-ups.

An adventurous congregation may well produce their own children's hymnbook with the much needed large print and illustrations. There are also a number of good professionally produced children's chorus and song books for those willing and able to spend money. Young children can also be excellent avenues for introducing new songs and choruses. Albeit with a high degree of sentiment and nostalgia, the elderly and more traditional will often readily accept something new from young children where they won't from the vicar. In time they may well grow to like the 'new' and receive happily what the children have to teach them.

Liturgy: Once again service cards and books add to the large load we carry into our services each week — our children being empty-headed. Many churches follow set patterns of worship if not large chunks of liturgy. If our children are to be expected to follow and understand these forms of worship they need at the youngest of ages to be helped through them. Simple home-produced service cards with the main items of the liturgy in large print, preferably with illustrations, can make a real difference to a little one's understanding and involvement in the liturgy. They can even be carefully handwritten and photo-copied.

For some years before they could read, our own twins loved to look at the brightly coloured children's communion booklet produced by Mowbrays. We gave every person in the book the name of someone in our own congregation! They very quickly learnt to understand the different parts of the communion service. Incidentally the aspect they failed to understand most was why they, as followers or Jesus, were not allowed to share in this special meal. In desperation one week they decided to bring their own piece of bread from our breakfast table — consecrated or not they were determined to share in the body of Christ!

Reading: Bibles usually lie in the pews for people to use when following the readings during a service. Very few adults make use of them — perhaps the children will follow our example! The reading of the Scriptures in Jewish families was a very special time and also one of the most important parts of synagogue worship. The boys knew that they would have that great honour one day. In our services readings are often given a low priority. When children are present, especially, the reading should be carefully prepared, short and well read — possibly dramatically using the *Dramatised Bible*. Dull Bible readings give children a wrong feeling about God's Word.

There are so many wonderfully illustrated children's Bibles on the market today, both paraphrased versions and original texts, printed in large print and spaced out well enabling youngsters to follow the verses easily. With a brief introductory sentence to the lesson explaining a little of its background and context, many of the youngest children will be able to grasp the main story line and follow in their simplified versions. Better still, adopt one of these as a lectern Bible for use when the children are present. Above all choose a good reading — all ages enjoy a good story. That's why the Bible is full of them!

Prayers: There is little doubt that under fives were not intended to sit quiet and still for much longer than a minute, consequently the prayer time in a service becomes a parent's nightmare. When you are in a church where intercessions are long and formal it is probably best to make an exit beforehand. Ideally these should take place when the children have gone into their own groups, but if not equip yourself well with children's prayer and story books for use at this time alone. At one church they actually give out little drawstring 'Sunday' bags to all the under fives entering church. They contain several items including soft toys (without bells and rattles in them!), scrap paper, wax crayons and prayer books which are hardboard books suitable for the under fives. Parting with the bags can sometimes be a problem at the end of the service but it's well worth the effort and it can become a strong attraction for a return visit the following week.

For some general guidelines on leading young children in prayer, refer to chapter 3.6. These may be of help to those in charge of worship who are prepared to introduce simple prayers in a family service.

Instruction: One lives in the hope that no church expects children of any age to sit through a twenty-minute sermon. I am quite convinced that those who must endure such hardship are receiving regular inoculations against real Christianity though survivors expect others to go through it. Where there is no provision made for under fives, the only way to survive is probably to create a children's corner at the back of the church where parents can at least sit in a more relaxed way with their youngsters whilst they play hopefully quietly!

Increasingly, churches now extend the Sunday activities to incorporate the three-to-fives and run very effective creches for the under-threes so that parents can return to the main service and receive their instruction in peace. There are several excellent resources now available for the instruction of three-to-fives. Many of these can be found in chapter 7.11. The emphasis with this age group needs to be on learning through involvement and activity rather than sitting and listening — something that even adults struggle to do if they are honest. Perhaps we need to adopt a few of the learning methods for children in our own times of instruction.

Finally, we need to get the balance between involving under fives in the whole church family worship and avoid stretching their endurance to breaking point. Under fives need to go out as soon as the worship leader is unable to make concessions to that age group. This will probably be earlier than for older children who can join in. It is at this point that the creche becomes operative and therefore an essential part of any church family worship.

4.5 Guidelines for creches

One of my most vivid memories of our trip to America is the creche facilities at each church we attended. Having a husband who was always preaching and two very independent teenagers 'doing their own thing', I found myself week by week following the signs to the creche, or nursery as they frequently named them. What greeted me at the end of my search never ceased to amaze me. Our church back in England was fairly well organised when it came to the under fives, but the Episcopal Church certainly made us look like amateurs.

In almost every case there were several rooms available separating the 'sleepers', 'creapers' and 'toddlers'. Having two 'sleepers' by 10.30 a.m. I ventured towards the first, only to find between six and ten cots lining the room, each complete with clean white sheets and baby covers. Following an informal but thorough registration procedure I was introduced to the person responsible for my children and then gently persuaded to return to the service, assured that my babies would be well cared for and that I would be called immediately should they show signs of anxiety or distress. Changing, feeding and entertaining followed as a matter of course according to my specification at registration. The whole experience was a positive and welcoming one for both parent and babies.

A professional approach

Is all this really necessary? To go to such lengths and expense for just a few babies may seem just a little bit 'over the top'. Most of us concerned with Sunday creches are also involved with parent and toddler groups and feel that the organisation of these two groups is very much the same. The only very important difference lies in the fact that with a creche, leaders are totally responsible for the children in their care for the duration of time their parents are absent. This should seriously affect our organisation and structuring of a creche.

The majority of our creches probably run for up to an hour, rarely longer and often much shorter. It is worth remembering that once we exceed two hours we are in fact required by social services to be registered as a creche and have a suitably qualified person in charge. These are the regulations that apply to our playgroups and registered childminders. If on occasions we run creches for church family days or women's events which are likely to involve longer periods of time separating parents and children, we need either to timetable the programme carefully to no longer than two hour sessions, or go through the rather lengthy process of registration. The latter needs to be requested some three or four months in advance to be sure of getting through the red tape in time for the event.

Even the smallest of creches can aim for high standards. Whether you are welcoming three or thirty children and their parents, good organisation and facilities are essential. There will be inevitable practical restrictions as to the facilities we can provide as few of us have the enormous church complexes of the Episcopal Church, but nonetheless we need to be encouraged to make the very best of what we do have. May we also dare to suggest to our church leaders that this area of growth needs serious consideration when it comes to the allocation of rooms for the children's work as a whole. Sadly the creche is often bottom of the list and is allocated the entrance hall, porch or vestry — all of which are high unsuitable! Other important areas needing serious consideration when setting up a creche are those of leaders, registration and facilities. Guidelines on each of these are given below.

If parents are anxious about leaving their child in the creche for any reason, do encourage them to stay for a while. There is a very fine balance between forming a 'mothers' club' within the creche and accommodating the anxious mother. Seek to do the latter rather than the former, which tends to defeat the object of a creche facility. Many a meaningful conversation has taken place amidst the seeming chaos of babies and toddlers and we can be sure that God is as much at work there as he is in the main church service.

Guidelines for creche leaders

Aim for one adult leader to three children.

Try not to use too many of the young mums themselves who most need the opportunity to sit in church — or only use them on a helpers' rota basis.

Involve responsible teenagers, especially to play with the hyperactive two-year-olds.

Don't dismiss the possibility of male leaders. Not only are they good, but a male presence encourages dads to attend.

Ensure as much continuity in leaders as possible to help build up healthy trustworthy relationships with parents.

Have the same mature person 'in charge' and completing the registration procedure each week so that parents and children become familiar with them.

Allocate babies and children to specific leaders to be responsible for them until parents return.

Make sure there is someone free to leave the room to fetch parents if necessary.

Guidelines for creche registration

Give a warm welcome to new families.

Try not to be too formal about this but be sure to obtain basic details of new families, e.g. name, address, age and date of birth of baby.

Introduce parents to the leader responsible for their child.

Label each child, preferably on their back with a sticky label, not pins of any description.

Indicate on the label any special needs, e.g. 'milk allergy', 'no biscuits', 'feed at 11am' etc.

Label pushchairs and prams if several are alike.

Label babies' bottle or feeder cup if they bring their own.

Make a note of where parents are sitting in church.

Reassure parents that they will be called if needed.

Guidelines for creche facilities

Consider the needs of the differing age groups.

'Sleepers' may require cots or prams, baby slings or bouncing cradles.

'Crawlers' require safe floor surfaces, preferably carpet or large rugs and floor cushions, and soft toys, building bricks and other suitable toys to play with.

Toddlers require space and as many varied toys and activities as you can provide.

Toilet facilities within easy reach are essential, not forgetting an endless supply of disposable nappies and cleaning-up materials.

Refreshments can be useful but do ask parents' permission beforehand and respect their decisions.

Aim for high standards of hygiene at all times by regularly washing soft toys and blankets. Keep a sterilising unit available for dropped dummies and feeding bottles if necessary.

Safety should be a high priority. Ensure that toddlers can't escape and that all sockets, switches and heating appliances have protective guards or cover. Never let children leave a creche unless they go with the adult responsible for them.

4.6 Building on baptism, thanksgiving and dedication contacts

Few young families attend church as a matter of course in our present day. More usually they come in through contacts with Christians outside the church (which is of course the basic argument put forward in this book). The one exception is in the area of requests for a service of thanksgiving (for the birth of a baby), infant baptism (in the Anglican and Methodist church), and a service of dedication in most nonconformist churches. The building on these contacts needs to start before any of these services actually takes place.

A time for preparation

Increasingly, churches are becoming aware of the need to educate and prepare parents of young babies for the steps they are about to take in any of these services. The prayers they will offer and in some cases the promises they are to make should not be taken lightly. Time spent with each family can become a valuable opportunity to express concern for them and the spiritual wellbeing of their child. Many parents welcome this time and value the instruction and guidance given in Christian parenting.

As an Anglican church we make a special effort to spend time with our young families in this way and it is largely the parents themselves within the church that do this important work. The clergy make sure that we are all well trained and taught in the theory of baptism and we are helped along by the CPAS 'Square One' baptism preparation kit. This is one of several aids that are available in this field. This particular kit includes a video presentation explaining the meaning of both the services of thanksgiving and baptism. A very high percentage of homes now own video recorders and where they don't we take one along for the visit.

The service itself

In our own church we aim to make services of baptism as warm and welcoming as we possibly can. A member of the baptism team greets families at the church door and seats are reserved for them and friends at the front of the church. Candles, cards and certificates are given as permanent reminders of this special day. The full congregation including the children remain in church for the duration of the service as a sign of the welcome that we are extending. On occasions a very special song is sung for each baby and they are handed over to a member of the church to symbolise the acceptance into the family. The vast majority of these families are moved by the love, friendliness and personal touch of the whole service.

It always seems incredibly sad to me to hear of any of these services taking place in isolation from the church family in an afternoon or following a morning service. For some churches it is the only way they can cope but it makes a farce of any of the prayers of welcome or acceptance into the church family when there are no representatives from the church other than the minister or vicar.

Following up the families
For many families any one of these services happily marks the start of their regular church attendance. For others it can be difficult, and of course there are always those who never had any intention to take seriously their commitment to Christian parenting. Pressurising families into attending church is counter-productive but there is no reason why prayers cannot continue for that child and acknowledgement of the anniversary of the service be made. Some churches choose to remember the child's birthday, others the anniversary of the service, but whichever it is they are included in what is often called the 'cradle roll'. Cradle rolls require good administrators as they can quickly get out of date with frequent changes of address and additions to the same family.

One of the most helpful aids to baptism follow-up that I know is the 'One to Five' preschool Christian nurture pack. As well as guidelines on child development and various hints on successful follow-up, it includes five of the most delightful professionally produced coloured cards. They can be ordered apart from the pack in multiples of five from The Mother's Union.

When we moved to our present parish the family services were very different from those in our previous church — naturally so. For a few weeks our twins struggled with the change until gradually my husband injected his natural humour and respectful informality into the worship. Children seemed to emerge from everywhere. Some months later a very small girl wandered quite freely and happily up to the front of the church during a hymn and whispered into my husband's ear, 'I want to wee...' Nobody in the congregation batted an eyelid — least of all the tiny tot herself. The church seats nearly 2,000 when full and to a two-year-old must seem enormous. To be sufficiently confident to wander up to a six-foot-three-inch vicar dressed in robes in front of 300–400 people must say something for the welcome that child felt.

This small but meaningful incident did more to encourage us in our early days in this parish than that little girl will ever realise. We thank God for the ministry of the under fives in every shape and form!

Part Three
EVANGELISM
THROUGH EVENTS

Introduction —
Are We Ready?

Evangelism is a very topical subject. In the Church of England we have all been called to a decade of it. If you had asked me ten years ago to describe what I though evangelism involved I would have probably given you a very narrow answer. Then the title would have conveyed the idea of something very rigid and clinical — a time when set questions would be asked and set replies given regardless of the understanding of those involved. There would have surfaced within me memories of a certain type of evangelism programme to which I was introduced in my youth when questions were drilled into me and very definite responses memorised in preparation for the street work we were engaged in as young people.

I remember one particular occasion in a London Park when I was determined that the poor chap I'd stopped was going to get the full benefit of my recently acquired knowledge and witnessing technique. (After all I had spent a full week learning it.) Imagine how I felt when some minutes later, as I stopped to take a deep breath, the dear man said, 'How lovely, my child. I also know my peace with God through the Lord Jesus Christ and have done so for some 35 years now.' What a gracious man to have allowed me to finish my onslaught!

Despite my youthful naiveté I have to say that the training I received in those days is probably one of the most useful things I have ever acquired. I draw upon that knowledge and skill time and time again. I learnt how to explain the basics of my faith using my Bible, how to respond to some of the difficult questions that might be asked, and how to lead someone through to a point of personal commitment to Christ. Above all it left me with a lasting conviction of the need to be prepared for and bold in my witness.

(There are a number of excellent resources available for training individuals and groups in the task of personal evangelism. Some of them are listed in chapter 7.6).

Clearly what I did lack in those early days was a sensitivity towards and an understanding of the people I was sharing with. I hope that age and experience have since taught me something of those important qualities. The sharing of our faith should not be a rigid and clinical technique that we launch into as and when we please. It should arise out of a deep compassion for people and a desire to see them touched by the love of God.

Jesus had sensitivity and compassion towards individuals and situations. His witness was a natural and spontaneous part of his conversations with people. His meeting with the Samaritan woman at the well, as recorded in John's Gospel, chapter 4, illustrates this beautifully.

Firstly, he found a common interest and shared with her. The first and most amazing thing about this meeting was that Jesus bothered to speak to this woman at all. Jews didn't speak to Samaritans and Rabbis certainly didn't speak to women of ill repute! But they had something in common — the need for water — and Jesus was not going to let the attitudes of others stop him from speaking. It turned out to be an excellent foundation for what was to come.

We too in our under-fives groups may find ourselves speaking with those whom society rejects or finds difficult to cope with. The single parent, unmarried mother, abused wife or child, sufferers of Aids, those from other cultures and religions, underprivileged families, the depressed and lonely will at some time come into our groups.

We have the privilege of sharing in people's lives, of discovering common interests. As a baby is born, as a child grows and develops, as relationships are strengthened and family life enjoyed, we have many excellent foundations on which to build our conversations about God, our evangelism. Of course not all of these foundations will be happy ones. We will encounter problems and needs just as Jesus did.

Secondly, he spoke of her need — but didn't go too far. The Samaritan woman's greatest need was a spiritual one — Jesus could clearly see that. But rather than announcing to her who he was and what she ought to do in order to 'be saved from her sin', he gently and sensitively aroused her interest and told her as much as she was ready to understand. He only revealed his identity when she was ready to receive it and the response was amazing. She hurried off to tell the whole town what had happened to her!

The needs of the families we come into contact with are many. And the gospel we have to offer is 'good news'. As Isaiah puts it, in chapter 6.1 verse 1, we are

> To bring good news to the poor,
> To heal the brokenhearted
> To announce release to captives
> And freedom to those in prison.

Material poverty is a daily reality for many of us working in the cities but spiritual poverty is in abundance everywhere we look. The broken hearts of parents and children alike walk into our groups daily seeking healing and wholeness. Others remain captives and prisoners to materialism and greed in the self-centred world in which we live.

We have a gospel to proclaim, Good News to share, for a world that desperately needs to hear it. These people don't need condemning. They need loving, their interest arousing, and leading on in their understanding until they are ready to be challenged with the true identity of Jesus.

Thirdly, He was persistent and didn't get side-tracked. All through his conversation with this woman Jesus stuck to the main issue. At one stage she was ready to side-track him with questions about Israel's history, but Jesus brought her back to the point — the challenge. Was she or was she not going to believe what he said? She had to decide for herself if he was the Messiah. There was no missing the point.

As we share the Good News of Jesus — his love, his acceptance, his forgiveness and the New Life and hope that we can find in him — we too will need to be persistent and not get side-tracked. There will be many times when people try to put red herrings before us.

As Christians we won't have all the answers, we don't always understand why certain things happen. Our own lives are not free from pain or tragedy. One thing that we are not offering is an insurance policy against all life's problems. But we do offer somebody who will help them face life with hope and purpose. We need to concentrate on that person — Jesus. It is his words and claims that will speak the loudest.

We must be clear about the challenge we are presenting. It is not about clocking up numbers into our church services. I say that because it was something that God spoke quite clearly to me in the early days of my work with under fives. 'Bring the people to Me,' were the words I found repeatedly going through my mind. The challenge is to respond to Christ not the demands of the local church! True, one hopes that new Christians will become part of the local body, but the danger is that once in church they become sucked up into a whirlwind of church activity before really understanding anything of what they have come to, and finding God himself.

It would be nice to think that our every conversation leads to a positive response to Jesus. That may have happened to you but it's not an everyday experience for most of us. It often takes time to share with our families and establish common ground. It takes time to share in people's lives, to discover and respond to needs. And being persistent may mean keeping on in prayer and testimony for months, even years.

The most important thing of all is that we are ready, willing and wanting to evangelise — to share our faith. It will be our personal experience of Jesus, his love, forgiveness, and wholeness that speaks the loudest. We can learn texts, acquire helpful skills for presentation and try out all kinds of new ideas, but without our own personal experience to draw upon all of that will sound empty.

Are you ready?

5

Faith-Sharing Events

The sharing of our faith is an integral part of the sharing of our lives in everything we say and do. But it can also take place within an organised event or group set up for that specific purpose. This chapter looks at three different ways of setting up such events and the practicalities of leading them.

Sooner or later the sharing of our faith will involve us in some sort of presentation of what we believe and have experienced. It is at this stage that the limitations of the surroundings of an under-fives group can be most frustrating. For many of us it takes some courage to get to the point of sharing our own Christian testimony, and having done so there can be little more distracting than having to stop to take young Lucy to the potty or prevent James from murdering his sister in one blow! If meaningful and effective discussion is going to take place is requires some time and space where issues can be thought through and discussed — not easily found in a playgroup, parent and toddler group or even a church service.

By planning a specific event, a series of group discussions, or even a structured course you are creating opportunities for numbers of people to hear and consider something of your faith. There may be much discussion and debate, rejection and acceptance but all of this is a valuable part of people's personal spiritual pilgrimage. Their spiritual journey will hopefully become a time of great discovery made possible because of our various faith-sharing events.

5.1 Choosing the best type of event

If you have never set up or led a faith-sharing event before, be sure to pray and plan well in advance. I would encourage you to spend weeks praying and listening before you make any firm decisions. It can be helpful to record your responses and reactions over this period of time and perhaps compare them with a prayer partner's. This stage of the Holy Spirit's leading and guiding is very important and it can often prove very interesting to see how your thinking changes as a result of on-going prayer.

It is important that you choose the right type of event or group for your situation. Be governed by the degree of spiritual awareness amongst your families and their receptiveness to Christian things. You may need to 'sound out' one or two folk by asking them if they might be interested in coming along to a special evening event or a daytime discussion group. Be honest about the level of understanding of God that your families have and aim to build on it. Many will not be ready to consider, say, a course in basic Christianity, but they may well be interested in hearing the testimony of a Christian who has gone through the experience of miscarriage or child bereavement. Above all pray that God will guide and lead you at this vital stage of your thinking.

5.2 Considering the options

Over the years I have been involved in a number of different faith-sharing events set up especially with parents in mind. The simplest was the testimony spot within a parent and toddler group session as described in chapter 1.6. Others have been separate events that demand a lot of preparation and organisation. Many of the practical aspects of setting these up will be discussed later. But first let's look at three different types of event and the choice of materials for them. A list of resources and suppliers of these materials can be found in chapter 7. The list is by no means exhaustive.

5.3 An occasional 'special' event

An occasional 'special' event is what it says it is — an event which is neither usual in content or regular in occurrence. It's special and occasional!

Many under-fives groups incorporate such an event into their programme just once or twice a year. They boldly but sensitively present something of the Christian faith in a positive and relaxed atmosphere. An occasion of this kind aims to arouse interest, and to cause parents to stop, think and hopefully take God a little more seriously than they did before. The parable of the sower illustrates what such an occasion may achieve. The seed is scattered and falls on very different grounds. The people present will all be at different stages in their thinking. The truth about God that we offer will be received differently by each person present. The important thing is that we are aware and observant, ready to nurture any growth that does take place. For some it may be the first time they have ever thought about God, for others the realisation that God is someone they can know, and for others a time when they are deeply convicted of personal sin. God is at work at every stage.

Some make an event of this kind into a very attractive occasion which includes a light lunch or supper. If you try this be careful not to be carried away and forget the central purpose of the meeting. Plan carefully so that the 'faith-sharing' bit remains the priority and do be honest in your advertising. Do not get people along under false pretences. It may be helpful to issue tickets, especially where there is a charge made for food. It also serves to indicate the numbers to expect. If there is any fundraising element, again, keep that as a fun 'extra', not as the central purpose.

Since numbers are likely to be higher than at a group which runs for some weeks, the occasion requires material that is able to stand completely on its own with little introduction and which stimulates thought and discussion easily.

Content/material suggestions

Using a good speaker or speakers is ideal for this type of event, that's if you can find them. Be sure that you either know them yourself or have them recommended by someone you trust. One of the most fruitful occasions we ever had in our last parish was when a couple of evangelists (man and wife) came to share simply what God had meant to them as parents when their children had been growing up. It was a daytime event so we ran a creche and laid on good coffee and nice biscuits! But speakers do not always need to be 'professionals'. There are many untapped resources in our own church congregations especially amongst the members maturer in years. They often have a lifetime's experience of God to share.

It can be useful to link these occasions in with Christian festivals. Consider an evening preparing for Christmas with cooking, present-making, singing and a speaker talking about the true meaning of Christmas. Similar events can be planned with Easter and Harvest in mind. Mothering Sunday also provides an excellent common ground from which to talk. Think of inviting several Christian mothers all with different experiences to share about their lives and faiths. You may even have a 'famous' mother in your region with a very special story to tell.

If you are really 'on the ball' you can pick up on current issues and address them through a speaker or a panel of speakers. 'The evidence for the resurrection' when the Bishop of Durham was in the news would have provided an ideal opportunity. The church and religion generally are often portrayed negatively through the media. We need to turn these news stories into positive opportunities.

Another possibility for this type of event is the showing of a Christian video. They can be easily obtained and there are an increasing number of well presented Christian videos available. Sunrise Videos produce two particularly suitable programmes. *Somebody up there loves me* is a 25-minute film which tells of four people's different accounts of how and why they became Christians. All four come from inner city and working class areas. *Journey into life* is also 25 minutes and features Cliff Richard and mime artist Danny Scott. It gives a clear and sensitive presentation of the gospel.

Bagster Video produce one of the bestsellers called *Mine to Share*, once again featuring Cliff Richard in a two-tape presentation of his challenge to young people. It is designed for youth but not unsuitable for young parents.

It is essential to view the video yourself at the planning stage and decide how you are going to use it.

As well as these direct gospel presentation videos there are a number of very challenging films about individual Christians' experiences. They can be excellent and are certainly memorable. Popular ones include the story of American Joni Eareckson who struggled against quadriplegia following a diving accident; *The Hiding Place* telling a powerful testimony of a Christian woman facing intolerable conditions and persecution during World War Two, and the well known *Chariots of Fire* which of course has been screened in our national cinemas and on television. They are not suitable for immediate group discussion but may stimulate useful conversations afterwards or later.

You may be thinking that all these videos cost a fortune to buy. It is true that they rarely cost under £9, but large Christian bookshops, diocesan and other resource centres increasingly offer them for hire. A fee is usually charged. A few large national companies have also started video libraries from where films can be hired. Some of these are listed in chapter 7.5.

Leading the 'occasional' event
The leading of this type of event is likely to be quite different from that of the smaller on-going series of group meetings. Whilst many of the points on leading small groups (covered later in this chapter) are relevant, there will be certain key differences that need to be taken into consideration.

Firstly, it is likely that the numbers at such a broader, more social occasion will be higher. (Remember that this does not need to be an evening — I know of several very successful lunch-time occasions.) It will demand more 'up front' confidence than a small informal group. But don't be daunted by the task. Prepare and practise in advance what you are going to say.

Secondly, there will be a much wider range of attitudes and opinions and you may well encounter some negative and antagonistic responses. Be prepared to take this. It can be very healthy and be part of a necessary process through which some people have to go if they are to believe. But you must stay in charge of the event. ·

Thirdly, the atmosphere created and image projected on these occasions are critically important. It is these things that will leave a lasting impression in people's minds. Too often on such occasions the Christians are fighting to be in the kitchen or absorbed in 'doing' rather than in 'being'. Our friendliness and willingness to mix and chat with folk are vital.

A positive and definite welcome will help people feel warmly accepted whatever their belief or disbelief. Encourage them to be open-minded and free to express their opinions without causing offence. Whatever you do, don't apologise for what you are doing in presenting the Christian faith in the way you have chosen.

Fourthly, it will not be so easy to direct a discussion time on these occasions. Smaller informal groups where people have built up trust and confidence in each other are the ideal. But if you do decide to have an open discussion time, prepare well and try to anticipate the issues that will arise. Take control especially if the numbers are high. Alternatively break down into smaller discussion groups with prearranged sub-group leaders following the guidelines suggested above.

5.4 A series of events — based on discussion topics

Approaching our faith via a particular subject or topic is not an easy way out. We are not trying to avoid presenting the gospel or sharing our faith. If anything it is harder, as it requires us to face and think through issues that as Christians we'd sometimes sooner ignore. Then we need to be able to express those thoughts and opinions.

In my early student days a man by the name of Von Daniken wrote a series of books on the subject of space and life in space. One of his theories was that God was a spaceman. Students all over the country seemed to be soaking up this literature like sponges. A Christian tutor at a nearby university agreed to give a lecture on the scientific evidence backing this man's theories — or rather the lack of it. We took several of our unbelieving friends along and it was the beginning of their taking Christians and God seriously. They would never have attended a Christian Union meeting but because we were offering them something that they could relate to they responded.

As I write this very chapter, the well known Bishop of Durham had yet again made public his very personal views on the physical resurrection of Christ. Whatever we may think of those views, it had become a High Street shops and local pub topic of conversation. We need to take advantage of such opportunities to talk about our faith in the risen Jesus. More often on such occasions you find the Christian population retreating into their holy huddles to debate the issues instead of getting out into the world and debating them.

It is important that we are in touch with the world and the issues that face people daily. Too often we live in a vacuum, burying our heads in the sand and pretending that the harsh realities of life don't exist. This is particularly the case when it comes to issues relating to women. We desperately need to acknowledge what is happening and begin to act as the salt and light in the world that Jesus intended us to be. God has much to say to people who struggle with relationships and with financial and educational disadvantage. He longs to be the voice of the losers in society. But those who are 'advantaged' are no less in need of the gospel. Women and families of wealth have personal, family and work issues to face also.

So to share our faith through topical issues is far from side-stepping reality. It is taking God into the world in a very real way.

There are so many areas that could be covered in this way and some lend themselves more obviously to a strong and direct Christian input. Where you deal with a very specialised subject such as 'Living in a multicultural society' or 'Your child and education', it is probably best to invite a speaker who can deal confidently with the issues that may arise. Finding Christians who can speak on these topics (especially for a daytime meeting) may take some time and certainly you need to make sure they are available several months ahead of the meeting.

I have tried to suggest below topics and issues that are relevant to young families, particularly women. Relevant resources including names and addresses of support groups and organisations can be found in chapter 7. The leading of small groups will be discussed later in this chapter.

Topics for discussion

- Discipline and the under fives
- The development of your child's personality
- Childhood bereavement
- Miscarriage
- Coping with post-natal depression
- Childhood illnesses
- Children with special needs
- Why baptise your child?
- Aids
- Living in a multi-cultural age
- Women in a changing world
- Marriage difficulties
- Women's health

- Starting school
- Education and your child
- Single parenting
- Working mothers and wives
- Choosing child care

5.5 A course in basic Christianity

Over the last ten years it is the basic Christianity course that I have used more than anything else as a faith-sharing event. It never ceases to amaze me just how open people are to discussing the existence of God and the claims of Jesus and how willing they are to come to a group where they are sure that you are not going to subject them to hours of indoctrination but allow them to express and explore opinions for themselves.

There are several excellent courses available for the genuine enquirer, and some are described below. Nearly all of them are backed up with good clear discussion material, making your own job as leader a lot easier. They are specifically designed for faith-sharing purposes but can also be used to clarify or renew the faith of a believer. Even though I have used some of these time and time again, I still find them absorbing and challenging.

Some Courses for Enquirers

Christian Foundations is an eight-week course on audio cassette in two parts. Each four-week part can be used independently. David Watson speaks for about 10 minutes in response to very basic questions about the faith. Questions for group discussion are included.

Jesus Then and Now consists of twelve 20-minute video presentations exploring the life of Jesus and how that life can affect us now. Once again

---

David Watson speaks on this subject, and groupwork is available to follow up the programmes.

Good News Down Your Street is a basic down-to-earth examination of the Christian faith through discussion and Bible study. It comes with an instruction booklet and cassette tape describing ways in which the course has been successfully used.

SEAN — Abundant Life Course is a course designed to teach people how to live as Christians. Available with it is a helpful booklet containing guidelines and discussion starters for use specifically with young parent groups. Used in this way it lends itself to evangelistic purposes.

5.6 Leading faith-sharing groups

'What me?' some of you may say. The thought of actually leading such an event may never have crossed your mind. Being involved with the practical side of setting up an event and perhaps even contributing to the discussion is one thing, but to actually lead is something else!

The temptation is strong to bring in the 'professionals' when it comes to the hard bit of answering difficult questions and leading discussion. Perhaps the vicar or minister, curate or lay reader — anyone but me. The fact is that you are the professional in this situation. You are the ones who have done the ground work, the ones who understand your group, the ones who speak their language. So why complicate the matter by bringing in someone who is unknown to them and has little in common with them? In groups ministers tend to be regarded as 'the experts' and instead of discussion it can become a lecture. By all means enlist the support and guidance of your minister or leader and bring them in if you require their expertise one week on specialist subject areas, but otherwise be confident in yourselves and get on with the job of leading the groups yourselves. You can do it!

5.7 Practicalities

You will take a lot of the anxiety out of leading if you organise the practical side of things well and in advance. You will need to decide the best form of publicity. It can range from personal invitations to a general distribution of leaflets advertising the group. If you intend to have them professionally printed do allow plenty of time.

If your group is a daytime one and needs a creche, get your leaders/helpers arranged early and make sure that the facilities are of a high standard. If in doubt about setting up a creche refer to chapter 4.6 which deals with creche on Sundays, as the same principles apply. A checklist of other practical points is given below.

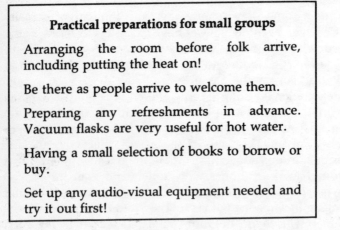

Practical preparations for small groups

Arranging the room before folk arrive, including putting the heat on!

Be there as people arrive to welcome them.

Preparing any refreshments in advance. Vacuum flasks are very useful for hot water.

Having a small selection of books to borrow or buy.

Set up any audio-visual equipment needed and try it out first!

Photocopy any handouts you may require.

Be prepared for the fused plug, blown projector bulb, run-down batteries and any other possible breakdown that may occur.

You can't anticipate everything that could go wrong. When arranging a training day a few years ago I really did think that I had allowed for every possible eventuality. We were expecting 78 children in the creche and had taken over the local baby clinic to accommodate them. Everything was arranged well in advance and then less than an hour before they were all due to arrive there was a power failure in the building! The devil will try anything! Several of us gathered to pray at the communion rail and heat and light were restored just in time.

5.8 Preparing your material
Whatever the topic or materials you choose, do familiarise yourself with them thoroughly. Whether it's a video, audio cassette, or Bible study outline, immerse yourself in it so that you can lead and contribute with confidence. If a topic, read up on it as much as you can. Don't depend entirely on the discussion material that you have been given. Adapt it according to your needs and if necessary produce your own outline and list of questions. In preparing ask yourself:
- Will they understand this question? Does it use religious words that they may not understand?
- What might they say in response to each question? Try to anticipate areas of concern or objection.
- How can I illustrate this particular point to help them understand?
- How can I re-word questions to encourage discussion instead of one-word answers?

If you are relaxed, others will usually relax. Try to keep the group moving in a positive direction. If you have invited a speaker to talk on a particular subject ask him or her well in advance to suggest discussion starters or questions. Offer to lead or at least chair that time so that the speaker can relax a little after speaking and listen to people's discussion. Don't presume a readiness to be subjected to an open question time — always ask beforehand.

5.9 Leading a discussion

On most occasions, with perhaps the exception of the 'occasional' event where the numbers are often higher and the aim broader, aim to create an atmosphere where people can express and explore opinions freely. Maximum time needs to be created for discussion. Leading a discussion time is a skill which can be acquired gradually with a few guidelines and plenty of practice. A list of guidelines is given below.

Guidelines for leading discussion

Limit the group to no more than 7–8 people, splitting into two smaller groups for discussion if necessary — preparing sub-leaders in advance.

Arrange chairs so that you as leader can see everyone and vice versa.

Never outnumber the enquirers with Christians. A ratio of 3 to 1 is about right.

Remember that a discussion is every-member participation, not a monologue from you or a dialogue between two people.

Try to anticipate some of the common areas of objection, e.g. the problem of suffering in the

---

world, creation versus evolution, the church as an institution, the authority of the Bible.

'Earth' the questions as much as possible, relating them to familiar experiences and situations.

Don't be afraid to encourage quieter members of the group to join in by simply asking, 'Do you agree with what is being said?' or 'What do you feel about this, Jane?'

Prepare open questions that demand an opinion or series of thoughts, and avoid one-word answers, i.e. closed questions. Be careful not to reject individuals because you disagree with their opinions. Thank them for being open and honest about what they think and invite another response.

Beware of red herrings and have the courage to put the discussion firmly back on course if they do appear.

You won't have all the answers and so don't be frightened to say that you don't know. However, do find out if you possibly can for the next time.

Always try to end the discussion on a positive note, particularly if it has been 'heated'. Allow people to wind down, perhaps injecting a little humour to relax everyone.

5.10 Structuring your time

If you are leading a daytime event, its length will be largely determined by the children. Evening groups do allow a little more time (but have the usual complication of everyone having to find babysitters). However long a session you are able to have, it still requires careful structuring to gain maximum benefit from the time. If the main input is a tape of some sort, either audio or visual, it will probably absorb between 15 and 25 minutes. If a speaker is invited, ask them to tailor their talk to no more than 20 to 25 minutes as it becomes hard to concentrate beyond that and there is a danger of over-running into valuable discussion time.

The start and finish of group times are very important. Your aim at the beginning is to welcome and relax people, and at the end to send them away thinking positively and wanting to return. Do try to be firm and disciplined about timing even at the risk of appearing a little bossy — it's worth it in order to achieve what you set out to do. If you are unreliable on time-keeping people may stay away.

In your introduction, explain how the group will develop and generally set the scene for that session, so people will know what will happen. Give a brief opportunity for anyone to ask questions at this stage concerning the structure in case they are anxious about anything. Reassure them if they do appear worried. At the very first meeting you may need to spend more time relaxing and getting to know people in order to lay good foundations of trust and friendship from the outset. This is time well invested. It can be a good idea to set the ball rolling by introducing yourself briefly and inviting others to do the same. Encourage them to say why they wanted to join the group even if it was because their best friend dragged them along. Humour is a tremendous relaxant if it comes naturally to you but if not, don't force it. I very often use true and funny stories about my own children or husband in order to get people laughing, and it also serves to show people I am a normal human being (something which some folk always doubt when it comes to clergy wives!).

At the end try to sum up what you have said and done. This is particularly important when things have turned out differently from how you expected. Be careful not to send anyone away upset or troubled in any way. If necessary talk to such people after the meeting. Also suggest anything that they may find interesting or helpful to take home and read, watch or listen to. Mention the subject for the next meeting so that the group can start thinking about it.

At the outset of your groups it will probably be inappropriate to pray but as time goes on you may feel that people would welcome prayer, particularly at the start and finish of the meeting. Advance slowly.

It is good to have an overall timetable in your mind even if you don't stick to it precisely. The danger of not giving yourself a structure is that unless you are very experienced and confident you will end up achieving little. A simple timetable based on a group running for one hour and twenty minutes is given below.

Suggested timetable for small groups

1.30	arrival time, settle children in creche
1.40	settle down into group perhaps serving coffee now
1.45	welcome and introduce topic of the day
1.50	listen to cassette tape
2.05	brief summary of what was covered on the tape
2.10	invite any immediate reactions before leading discussion
2.15	discussion time
2.55	draw discussion to a close
3.00	sum up and bring group to a close
3.05	leave some time for informal chatting
3.10	time to collect children

5.11 Difficulties you may encounter

There are bound to be problems that surface in various shapes
and forms as your groups progress. Some of the practical ones
have already been covered. Others can be healthy problems and
a natural part of the process of group development and being
involved in people's lives. Sometimes they surprise us and we
are not always prepared to cope with them. Here are some of
the things we have had to face over the years in faith-sharing
groups.

Disruption of children. Even the most well organised creche
cannot always handle the clingy child or one who feels unwell,
and therefore you may need to be prepared for a child being
present in the group.

Dominant and aggressive group members. These people are
extremely hard work and you may need to have a quiet word
with them suggesting that they give others a chance to speak.
Pray particularly for them and look for indications of the root of
their aggression.

Deep personal needs surfacing. It may be necessary to lead
someone from a group session. If they become very upset of
distressed the group may be able to help, but be prepared to
pass them on to someone able and experienced in counselling if
that seems appropriate.

Unsupportive partners. The majority of group members will
probably be women and some may have angry husbands at
home who are unhappy for their partners to be attending such a
group. Do be aware of the pressures you may be placing on
them. Encourage them to share with their partners what they
are discussing and feeling and then, as leaders, learn to pray for
the men as much as you pray for the women.

Do remember that the devil is alive and well and particularly
active in faith-sharing activities as it is the thing that he hates
most. Don't be surprised when problems arise — it is a sign that
he considers the work important enough to be attacked. We do,
however, need to put on our full armour in order to withstand

the attacks, so surround the individuals including yourselves with protective prayer.

5.12 Providing good back-up

Do make available as many different kinds of back-up resources as you can get hold of. Some group leaders may be able to pool their own Christian books, tapes and videos. Do be sure to label them clearly and have some sort of signing out book so that you can keep track of who has borrowed them.

There are a number of quite cheap booklets and leaflets available which are useful to give to people. Ask your church to buy these for the group. *Journey into Life* is probably the simplest and clearest of these. CPO also produce a wide range of excellent leaflets on various issues such as abortion, halloween, cults and sects, Aids, debt, sexuality, alcoholism, etc. They are well worth obtaining.

Good quality Christian magazines are also on the increase. *Christian Family* in particular deals with very topical issues for young families and makes both attractive and interesting reading. Whilst there are few who would sit down to read a book, many more will read a magazine.

5.13 Following up events

Whatever type of faith-sharing event you organise, you should always give thought to how you are going to build on the experience people have gained through it. Much will depend on the success of the event or on the development of the group over the period of time they have been meeting.

The well received 'occasional' event will perhaps prepare the ground for further events of this kind. It may also be a stepping stone to something more regular and structured. There may also be an opportunity to establish more personal links with one or two individuals who expressed particular interest.

When a discussion group has been meeting for some time, it may be appropriate to invite people to say how their thinking has changed and give the opportunity for those who are ready to make a conscious commitment to Christ. Some may well have reached that stage earlier but need the assurance and confirmation of telling someone. Be sure that each of you involved in leading have learned how to guide someone to that point of commitment using the Bible and, perhaps, a simple booklet.

Following up individuals is most important. It may range from simply praying regularly for an individual, to setting up a nurture group for several people who want to go on in their new-found faith. At some stage you will be faced with the task of integrating them into the life of the church. If your church is a vibrant, outgoing community of God's people, willing and happy to accept newcomers, your problem is small. On the other hand, if you are faced with nearly 400-year-old services in a language and culture quite foreign to your new believers — you have a problem.

Church can be a great culture shock to many young parents. It is quite likely that some have never crossed the threshold of the building before. Just entering a church can create a lot of anxiety. Not only that, Sundays are very often their one and only family day. We need to be aware of the pressures that we may be placing upon these people. In our last parish is was quite common for women to work on Sundays when their husbands were at home to look after the children. Employers have created the job market for these people, knowing full well the attraction of extra income, in some cases double pay.

How do we nurture the faith of these believers to cope with the many hurdles and obstacles of our post-Christian age? It is my firm belief that at first we need to provide that nurture to suit them. We cannot necessarily expect them to suddenly adopt a new lifestyle and routine just because it suits us and the church. For some this may mean that for a year or more these new Christians may be functioning outside of the Sunday congregations but within a regular nurture group. They may need initially to be encouraged to apply their faith among their family and friends, rather than abandon them for a Sunday service.

It is of course tempting to want to introduce all these folk to our services. In time they will be there, hopefully with their friends and families too. But until that time is right we have a responsibility to see that they receive all the friendship, fellowship, teaching and encouragement that they need. With those for whom church attendance is possible it is important to make sure the experience is, above all, enjoyable and spiritually rewarding.

Finally...
I would hate to give the impression that faith-sharing events can only succeed when organised in a particular way using certain structures and materials. I don't want to imply that there is only one way to do it. The first group of this kind that I ever led failed miserably to follow the guidelines suggested in the last few pages. That was because at that time I knew no better. The lessons learnt are the results of first-hand experience and painful mistakes.

I remember well the time the tape recorder broke down, resulting in my inflicting a 30-minute monologue on everyone — sending them all to sleep. Then there were the disastrous discussion times when the silences felt like nightmares. It took me weeks to accept that they really did not understand some of the words and terms that I was using.

I recall the young mum who stopped coming because she was terrified that I might ask her to read aloud and she could not. I only discovered weeks later. Another young Christian blamed the church for putting pressure on her marriage which finally broke and she turned her back on God as a result. I could go on and on recalling bad experiences, often caused through our own naiveté and inexperience. But at the same time by the grace of God many individual lives and families were touched and transformed by the love of God.

God sees the hearts of his people, and he takes what we have and uses it to draw others to him. We might not feel that we have much to offer in the way of expertise or skill, but the Holy Spirit is a wonderful counsellor and teacher. God only asks us to offer what we have and reminds us that 'My grace is all you need, for my power is strongest when you are weak' (2 Cor. 12.9).

Part Four
SUPPORTING
ONE ANOTHER

Introduction —
A Mother's Lifestyle

The majority of leaders of under fives groups are women. Perhaps that is to be expected since, apart from Sunday worship, most of the activities take place mid-week during the daytime. A high percentage of these women are also mothers of pre-school children. Others are usually older ladies who happily give of their spare time in assisting in the running of groups. A few are like myself who have continued in the work after their children have gone into full-time education.

Whatever your situation — a Christian mum simply attending a group with your child, both mother and leader, there for the benefit of your children and involved in the running of the group, or a leader free to get on with the job of leading without the anxiety of having your children around — it is imperative to understand something of the lifestyle and pressures of Christian mothers if we are to offer one another support and encouragement.

Motherhood came upon me rather suddenly. Not only did I become an instant mother to my two step-children on marrying my husband, I also managed to produce twins very soon after that. One year I was an independent and extremely active single teacher, and only 18 months later I was mother to four children! To be honest I didn't have a lot of time to sit around thinking about the change but the one area that I was desperately struggling with was my spiritual life. It seemed non-existent!

I took to writing letters to God at this time, and found it very therapeutic. Here is one I wrote when my step-children were aged ten and twelve and the twins just a few weeks old.

Dear God,

It's me again — you know — the one who emerges occasionally from the nappies and ironing to question and consult you on my latest trauma! It's a question today, Lord, quite a simple one really, not difficult for you to answer I'm sure. It's this — When exactly, Lord, should I have my early morning quiet time? (After all that is what I was taught at my discipleship class — rise early each morning and spend time alone with God.) Should it be after the 2 a.m. feed or the 6 a.m. feed? Or perhaps I should stay after the 10 p.m. feed seeing as it's usually past midnight before I crawl into bed!

Of course I am flexible and willing to change, Lord. Should I now find this time when the twins are having their morning sleep or afternoon nap and whilst the older children are at school? Perhaps then I'll be able to sit down and relax and meditate on your Word. You will answer the telephone and door for me during this time, Lord, won't you? And if I pray hard enough do you think that the cleaning and washing could... well... sort of disappear?! And if I fall asleep during this 'quiet' time will it still count?

I'm sorry to trouble you with all this, Lord, but I really need your guidance because I feel as if I'm getting nowhere fast! Please reply quickly and could you also tell me where my Bible is — you see I haven't seen it since the last time I read it. Don't worry about the Bible reading notes 'cause they're well out of date and it would depress me even more to see the January 3rd page open when it's now March 10th. My intentions were good, Lord — it was my New Year's resolution to stick to the daily notes and it did last three days!

    Hope to hear from you soon,
            Love, Judith

There were times during those demanding years when my letters to God were the only means of communicating with him that I could cope with. All my Christian life I had listened to talks and sermons on the absolute necessity of making your time alone with God a priority. 'If you're too busy to pray, you're too busy!' was a phrase that I took very seriously. But what happens when your 'business' is the lifeline of your children and husband? You can hardly stop feeding the baby, refuse to wash the nappies, and serve beans on toast for the third day running however good the nutritionists say they are.

What bothered me more than anything else was that nobody else seemed to have the same problem — or at least, as I discovered later, they weren't admitting to it! I could find little understanding or support from anyone. Even the church seemed to be saying to me, 'It won't last for ever — you'll be back into the swing of things when they're older and easier to have around.' I wasn't sure I'd survive until then.

I was rapidly ceasing to feel a person in my own right. I was always someone's wife or mother. People often intensified that feeling within me by asking me what I did or if I worked! You can picture the scene... Sunday lunch at the vicarage. Ten people sitting down to a full meal (served regularly when you're six to start with), and some bright spark asks, 'Do you work, Judith?

How I longed to reply, 'No, never. The house, dog, children, husband, telephone, callers, meetings all see to them themselves — I spend most of my time in bed!' But of course I never did find the courage.

On one occasion someone asked me, 'What were you?' as if I had ceased to exist in my present form! In hindsight I think that I should have replied, 'In my former life I was a cat!' just to see what sort of reaction I got. I laugh about these occasions now but at the time they were quite painful.

It was the word of God that became my lifeline. Certain verses are engraved upon my memory. God knew my circumstances, he knew everything that I did. He knew 'when I sit down and when I rise', and he does 'perceive my thoughts from afar' and is truly 'familiar with all my ways' (Psalm 139).

His promise to us is: 'Never will I leave you. Never will I

forsake you' (Hebrews 13.5).

God's love for us is neither determined by nor dependent upon one set time alone with him. Neither does he only speak to those who are at every church meeting. The 'still small voice' of God speaks to those who listen wherever they are or whatever they are doing. We need to learn to recognise that voice and practise living in his presence.

The realisation of these truths transformed my relationship with God as I sought to pray and listen at every possible moment in the day. Prayers were said at the nappy bucket and ironing board. The Bible was kept open amidst the paint and glue (I acquired a new one as soon as the twins went to school!), and God taught me to listen and learn, pray and reflect through the everyday incidents of life.

Now my life has much more order and routine to it, but I treasure those days of real spiritual discovery and closeness to God, despite the fact that the number of undisturbed times alone with him were few.

Knowing and feeling our security in God are so important as we engage in his work. We need all the understanding, support and encouragement that we can get from each other and from our churches. Praying together, learning to lead together and educating the whole church family so that they too will understand and support are all vital parts of supporting one another.

6

Praying, Leading
and Church Support

The task of supporting one another is the responsibility of everyone. This chapter suggests practical ways of praying together, leading, and enlisting the support of church leaders and members.

6.1 Praying
Having already acknowledged some of the difficulties faced by mothers in finding time to pray, how do we set about this essential task? When you are determined to pray it is amazing where and how you can do it.

6.2 Pray anywhere and at any time
Personal prayer can be said at the ironing board or kitchen sink, so why not the church kitchen or porch for corporate prayer? Praying as you sweep the floor, wash up cups or put away the toys is better than not praying at all. Too often we wait for the right moment or right words and they never quite come. Many a time we have stood together as leaders and stumbled out a one-sentence prayer only seconds before an invasion of mothers through the doors. Don't be put off by the presence of your children at such times — simply tell them who you are talking to and why. Prayer times don't need to be long and arduous as God is very good at understanding our mutterings. My most frequent prayer on such occasions was simply, 'Help.' God heard that one!

One of the most valued times of prayer for our own team was at the midweek service of Holy Communion. Older members of our Mother's Union would run a creche for just half an hour for us to enjoy the peace and tranquillity rarely found elsewhere. We would often extend this time to find just ten minutes when we could pray for each other's needs and the work of our various groups. This service is often one of the most neglected and poorly attended in the life of churches but it is a wonderful opportunity for mothers in particular to grab that which they most miss — quiet and stillness before God.

6.3 Pray in two's and three's
My own experience of trying to get half a dozen people together to pray is not encouraging. Arranging babysitters and finding a convenient time and place proved impossible. Far more practical and realistic was to meet in two's or three's. Each month we'd arrange to meet with another member of the team at least twice, to pray and share together about the work. Again this was often done with babies on the breast and toddlers at our feet but we did it. Over a period of six or more months it meant that each of us spent time in prayer with everyone in the team. This served to strengthen the bonds between us as leaders.

6.4 Pray in chains
Setting up a prayer chain was undoubtedly the most successful means of corporate prayer that we ever experienced as a team. The basic discipline of praying on a chain is as follows: receive your message, ring the message through to the next straight away, then pray. Our own pre-arranged times were always geared to the children's morning television programme in order to give us some time and space.

The chain is quite simple to organise but ideally requires everyone to be on the telephone. I do know however, of one prayer chain where members agreed to walk to the next person on the chain in order to deliver the prayer message — often praying on the way.

To set up a chain form a list of all those who want to be

included in the chain and place at the top the team leader who will be responsible for sending the regular messages down. (They too should be the recipients of any additional and urgent messages.) Give a copy of the list to every member of the chain, indicating where they come on it and who their next contact is. In the event of that person being out they can then simply follow down the list and keep ringing until they find someone at home. This is particularly important when the chain is used for emergency purposes and therefore calls are unexpected. A variation is for everyone to 'phone two people. This speeds up the process.

Many prayers were answered through our prayer chains. One in particular stands out in my mind. Our pram services were held monthly, and despite service cards with the dates on many simply forgot. It was Monday morning preceding the pram service. God seemed to be reminding me of one particular Mum called Julie. She had only been once before. I had no idea where she lived, or even her second name. So I had no means of reminding her. So down the prayer chain went the message, 'Pray for Julie, that she will come along today.'

That afternoon, in walked Julie. One of the team welcomed her saying how good it was to see her again and asking how she had remembered. 'Oh,' came the reply, 'I didn't! My little girl was watching Playschool (on television) this morning and came out to ask me if we could go to that church where they sang and danced! Then I looked for the card that you gave me last time and discovered that it was today.'

Coincidence? God used that little girl at the exact time the request to pray for Julie passed down the telephone lines. Five years late that same Julie heads up the parent and toddler team as well as being a member of the pram service team itself. God hears our prayers wherever, whenever and however they are said. And here he answered with a resounding 'Yes!'

6.5 All pray the same thing

How many times have you sat in a prayer meeting trying to pluck up the courage to pray and repeatedly going over in your mind what you might say? You are so preoccupied with your own planning that you have no idea what else has been prayed about before. I confess that I've done it often.

One of the advantages of having little time and space to pray is that when you do have it you become more disciplined. So you keep prayers shorts and simple. Everyone aims to pray the same thing. The prayer chain necessitates this discipline and can be particularly good training for those new Christians who find it difficult to pray aloud or with others.

When praying for a particular group it is helpful to give a structure for everyone to follow whether they are praying on their own or with others. Be quite specific and ask everyone to stick to it. I still receive the prayer card from our last parish's under fives work giving me specific things to thank God for and pray for each week. Knowing that between 30 and 40 others pray along the same lines gives a temendous sense of God's people praying in one accord.

Producing a prayer card or prayer and praise list is easily done with the aid of a photocopier. It can be distributed not only amongst the team but much more widely to the church leaders and congregation. (Be careful about including details that are confidential or personal.) The prayer support of our church is vital, as we'll see later in this chapter.

6.6 Make prayer available

Have you ever offered unashamedly and boldly to pray for any of the parents that you come into contact with? I'm not suggesting that you make a public announcement at the next toddler group meeting or accost someone with the words, 'You need our prayers.' There are ways in which you can make prayer sensitively and quietly available and you will be surprised at how a needy person so often welcomes that opportunity. They may not want you to pray with them but may simply request prayers for someone or something.

This is an opportunity for us to show love and concern for people and to become partners with God's Spirit in his work. But people need to know the opportunity is there. Put a small notice on a newsletter or place a prayer box somewhere in the room where people can drop in written requests. Or have a prayer board where people can write down their needs and know that they will be prayed for. Sometimes you may feel it appropriate actually to offer to pray with someone you know to be going through a difficult time, perhaps a marriage breakdown, bereavement or post-natal depression.

A few years ago God was speaking to me quite clearly about praying for the sick. I had attended a conference on healing, along with several others from our church. On returning home, as usual, because of my restricted circumstances I was unable to attend the services where we were learning as a body to pray and minister to those in need. So I decided that from then on I would offer prayer for the people with whom I did come into contact, i.e. the young families. I promised God that I would offer to pray for the first person that I spoke to who was sick or in need. For weeks I went round asking everyone how they were and to my amazement (almost unheard of in toddler groups) everyone appeared to be in the peak of health!

The weeks passed by and the memory of my promise faded with them, until one particular day I sat talking to a new mum. In the usual small talk I asked her which children were hers. 'That one,' she said, 'he's two and a half now.' She pointed in the direction of the slide. I saw a small boy attempting to mount the steps. He looked barely 18 months of age, never mind two and a half! Without hesitation this young mum began to tell me his medical history. Born some ten weeks prematurely he was found to have two holes in his heart and there was little hope that he would live. Weeks and months of surgery and intensive care followed as little Mark battled for his life with his Mum at his cot-side. Although he survived, the pressure and strain of all this bore heavily upon the couple's marriage, and eventually it broke leaving Pat to bring up her two small children alone.

As I listened to this traumatic account my heartbeat quickened and I was reminded of my promise to offer prayer for those who were sick. Every reason not to surfaced in my mind as I sat there: 'I dont know her well enough; she may not believe in anything; this isn't the time or place; what if she thinks I'm a religious fanatic!' I was greatly relieved when Pat got up to see to her children and I went out to make the coffee. Standing in the kitchen praying my usual one word prayer of 'help' I was overwhelmed with the sense of failure, I had missed my opportunity and let God down.

Minutes later Pat walked into the kitchen and there were the two of us face to face, no children around and absolute peace and quiet. It was now or never — God had given me another chance to do what I had promised. I can't remember exactly what I said. But as I started to tell her that I was a Christian and believed in prayer, Pat's eyes filled with tears. She looked at me and said, 'I've waited two years for someone to say that to me. A vicar prayed for Mark when we thought he was dying in hospital and it gave me hope and I believed that God wanted him to live. I've wanted someone to pray again for him ever since.'

You can imagine how I felt. Suddenly all my fears melted away, as I realised that all the time God had been preparing this family for my offer of prayer. We prayed with Mark and his family for weeks and months. The holes in his heart closed up and the expected surgery was not necessary. Although still slightly smaller than children of his age, he joins in everything that his peers do and is enjoying full-time school. Pat herself is studying hard at college in order to fulfil a life-long ambition to be a nurse. The whole family is now part of God's family and they are regular worshippers at the church.

Not all the families that we have prayed for as a team have

received such a happy and positive ending to their story. We have prayed for those facing the grief of cot deaths, broken marriages and miscarriages. We have cried to God for very sick children who have undergone major surgery both successfully and unsuccessfully. Many have been very confused and angry towards God. They have felt hurt and bitter about the pain and suffering they and their children have had to go through. Offering prayer isn't a recipe for getting what we want, it is asking God to enter and touch people's lives at a time when they most need him. Yes, he is a miracle worker, but he is also God and Sovereign, Lord over life and death. He calls us to pray and to love — the answers are in his hands. To be allowed to share in a family's suffering and pain is a privilege and one which we should not treat lightly.

6.7 Leading

If you asked fifty under fives groups what their greatest need is, I can almost guarantee that forty would say: leaders. I have certainly never heard of a group that has a surplus of helpers.

It would seem that the vast majority of under fives leaders are parents of small children themselves, who already have very demanding lifestyles. There is a limit to the amount of 'spare' time that any parent of young children has to offer. Sadly all too often keen and eager Christian mums over-commit themselves, leaving little time for their own children and families. I speak from experience!

It may seem strange that the writer of a book pointing out the importance and urgency of under fives ministry should suggest that leaders should limit their commitment. But years of experience has taught me that it is both foolish and counterproductive for parents to overload their schedule. We must each work out our own priorities and responsibilities and only take on what we know we can cope with. Once we have done this, we then need to respect and understand the varying degrees of time commitment that others have made and work within these limitations.

There will always be those times when pregnancy or unexpected sickness prevent us from fulfilling our commitments. On these occasions additional help may be needed. Anticipation is often the key here, and a few willing helpers ready to step into the breach for just a short period of time are a great help.

One of our pram service team was determined that the birth of her second child was not going to prevent her from attending the monthly service. We did insist that she was not on the rota for that month but she had every intention of being there. Baby Susannah had different ideas and insisted on being born on the day of the service — in hospital, I hasten to add! However both mum and baby were at the following month's service. I guess that is commitment of a rather special kind that assumes the blessings of good health and strength.

6.8 Leadership qualities

What spiritual qualities do we look for in a leader? Many of us responsible for leading teams would probably say that we can't afford to be fussy — we'll take anyone who wants to be part of the work. A genuine desire to be part of God's work is probably one of the most valuable qualities found in a leader. In the pram service chapter I highlighted three particularly important qualities: the desire to pray, a sense of commitment to the work, and a willingness to learn. Without these essential qualities a leader will be poorly equipped to face the task ahead. All the skills in the world won't make up for a lack of prayer, commitment and a desire to learn. But neither can we survive on these qualities alone. Under fives groups demand skills also and in some cases training and qualifications.

6.9 Leadership skills

Organisers, bookkeepers, typists, musicians, artists, cleaners and washer-uppers are just some of the skills welcomed by under-fives groups. Everyone has something to offer and there is always plenty to learn for those willing to do so.

Where parents are paying for a service, qualified workers are required. Understanding the importance of play, acquiring good administrative skills and helping children with special needs are a few of the areas in which some will need training. This is especially important in playgroups and the Pre-School Playgroups Association is the official body setting the standards and providing training courses. Details can be found through your local branch library.

It may be that there are parents or others amongst us who have many of these child-related skills and perhaps some who are professionally qualified. Granted that qualifications don't automatically make someone highly skilled in practice, it would however seem foolish to ignore this expertise provided that the person concerned can accept the Christian basis of the work. Clearly it would be unwise to ask non-Christians to lead teams, but one presumes they would not want to. They will have much to teach us and we should be willing to learn from them and in turn take time to share our faith with them.

6.10 Leadership training

One of the most effective methods of training someone is 'on the job'. Jesus gave us an ideal model for this in the way he trained the disciples. Firstly he showed them how the job should be done; then invited them to join him in doing it; and finally he sent them out to do it on their own. We need to adopt this model in the training of our teams. The process of learning is never easy and we need to make allowances for each other's inevitable mistakes. However, discovering new gifts and abilities can be exhilarating.

In desperation one day I asked an unemployed young woman if she would consider painting an old cupboard of mine which we desperately needed as a pram service resource cupboard. To my amazement and delight the result was a brilliant letterbox red cupboard covered in teddybears. We and the children loved it. She had never done anything like it before in her life. This was the start of years of superb artwork in story illustrations, posters, invitation cards, puppet designs and the leading of several workshops to assist others in the art of DIY design.

Some limited training is available from outside agencies. I have already mentioned the very professional work of the PPA who are undoubtedly the experts on the playgroup scene. Few Christian bodies have responded so far to the growing need for training and encouragement in this area. One that does, however, is the Church Pastoral Aid Society who have been running training days in the North of England. The first was held in Bradford in 1987 where over 130 delegates plus 78 children in the creche enjoyed a full day's teaching and workshops on the many areas relating to under fives groups. As a result of this event similar days, tailor made to meet local needs, were set up in Doncaster, Nottingham, Southport, Newcastle and Scarborough.

Such training days are quite demanding to organise, especially where the numbers of creche places required are high, but the encouragement and increased wealth of knowledge and training acquired through them is well worth the effort. CPAS are willing to help groups run such an event where they have a viable number and the right facilities. Details can be obtained from the central office.

The Mother's Union also have a department specifically for young families. On request they will supply various leaflets and resources for the work. Many dioceses also run special events for young families, some of which focus on training.

There are also many publications available which offer supportive literature, suggestions and ideas for working with the under fives. A full list can be found at the end of this chapter.

6.11 Leading the leaders

Whether you wanted to or not you may find yourself in the position of leading a team or even co-ordinating several different teams in an under-fives work. One of the dangers of being in this position is that you're tempted to do most of the work yourself. Do remember that the art of good leadership is delegation! You may have a lot of the good ideas but you will need to motivate other members of the team to carry them out.

An effective leader will always aim to work herself out of a job; she will encourage and enable others to such a degree that she no longer appears necessary. Before leaving our last parish I decided to work myself slowly out of all the various under fives groups that I had been working with. I would have been devastated if they had all folded up as a result of my leaving, as I would have realised that I had failed miserably! By the grace of God the work carried on and grew with new leaders becoming involved all the time. Some months later I popped into the toddlers group one day only to be met on the doorstep by a new leader saying, 'Hello, are you new here — come on in and I'll introduce you to another new mum who came today.' It was thrilling to know that this was the welcome that others were receiving.

One of the real privileges of being an 'enabler' is that, more often than not, you see people doing the things that you have taught and sometimes doing them far better that you did! At first this may feel threatening and you may well begin to wonder what you're there for now. But without your encouragement and gentle leading many gifts and abilities might go unobserved and unused. What a waste! Keep on encouraging and enabling as the leader of leaders.

6.12 Church support

Over the last ten years or so, I have on a few occasions had a phone call from a minister or vicar saying, 'I really want to use our playgroup (or toddler group) to serve the community and reach out to young families in need. How can I support and encourage the leaders?' These are calls I love to get and find easy to respond to. However, the more frequent cries have been from tired and weary Christian group leaders desperate to receive support and concern from their churches.

'What can I do to convince them of the value of this work?'

'How can we get them to pray for us?'

'They never show any interest in what we are doing!'

'Our work isn't considered spiritual — all the other children's groups get grants to assist their work and all we get is a charge for the use of the hall.'

So how do we go about enlisting the support of our church?

When the parent and toddler group started in our last parish over twelve years ago it rented a neighbouring church hall! High rents were endured along with poor heating, few leaders, a handful of toys, and little recognition from the church. It was a painful struggle. Today that same church accommodates over 200 families in its various under fives groups. A part-time family worker co-ordinates the work and her salary is paid by the church. One of her first tasks was to administer a £15,000 building project for the new playgroup, funded by the church. How did the change happen?

Needless to say there is no straight-forward solution or simple procedure, but as leaders we learned some hard and valuable lessons along the way. Here are a few suggestions that may help you to gain stronger support from your church for your work with under fives.

6.13 Making yourself known

This may be stating the obvious, but do remember that most of the Sunday congregation (including most of the leaders) do not see what goes on between Monday and Friday. Even those who absorb what is said in notices still remain ignorant as to who the toddler group or playgroup are and what precisely they do at 2pm on Wednesdays or whenever. You may feel that the church building is your second home but for the majority of worshippers the doors only open for an hour or two on Sundays. A child of one of our leaders was asked where she lived and replied, 'St John's Church'! I'm sure many of us must wonder at times why we don't take our beds with us.

It is to easy to jump to the conclusion that people don't care when in actual fact they don't know. So start with the obvious channels of communication — the weekly notice sheet, parish magazine, prayer sheets, posters, cards, etc. If you are adventurous produce a special leaflet introducing all your leaders, groups, activities. Plan an open day and invite members of the congregation. Better still, if you are courageous, ask for a spot in the service and tell people about the work. But be imaginative. Tell stories of the work. Interview a young parent and a child or play a tape of interviews with the children.

A few years ago our pram service team actually did a shortened version of a pram service during the main family service. The congregation was delighted and we had several volunteers come forward to offer their services. We were certain that this was as a direct result of their being able to 'see' what went on.

So set about the task of making yourself known. And plan to reinforce this at regular intervals — at least once a year — perhaps with an under fives Sunday.

6.14 Educating your church family
Making yourself known is just the beginning. Now starts the vital process of educating the people. Many congregations see under fives groups as simply somewhere for young mums to go. If the congregation is to offer real support and encouragement, they need to understand the importance of the work and grasp the vision as much as the leaders themselves.

The way in which we plan and present our work will determine how seriously the leaders and church body will take us. We need to be careful not to give cause for complaint and criticism. The work is hard and often physically demanding, but leaving the church kitchen in a mess or failing to sweep the hall floor will do little for our image and can in the long term only serve to hinder both relationships and the work as a whole.

Few groups actually find the courage to go to their church leadership and share the vision that they have for the work that they are doing. A vision can be highly infectious and it is important that as many people as possible catch it! So if they won't come to you, you go to them with your plans, prayer and publicity, and above all with your determination and enthusiasm. Ask to see your vicar/minister for an hour one day; go along to the church prayer meetings and visit home groups asking for their prayers and support, and then keep them in the picture.

I am sure that there were many times in our last parish when the folk wished that I had a topic of conversation other than the work of under fives! One Sunday evening after church we were hosting the Twenties and Thirties group at the vicarage. The majority were single but there were several engaged and courting couples amongst them. As usual I was trying to convince them that a certain under fives project was well worth supporting and praying for. One of the group was also the church treasurer and had an obvious 'concern' for the financial implications of what I was proposing. I remember saying, 'You see, I'm planning for the future — for when all you lot get married and have babies. You'll be grateful then for all our efforts now!' It was a bit presumptuous, I admit! However this very week I received a phone call to tell me that treasurer and his wife were expecting their first child. Out of the seven couples in the room that night they were the last to announce their news. The other six have all had their babies and are an integral part of the under fives work. Perhaps it was a prophetic word that night after all?! Your enthusiasm for under fives must be catching.

6.15 Asking your church family

What you don't ask for, you won't get! Don't be frightened to make your needs known and remember that requests don't always have to be financial. Some needs can be met directly, for example, secondhand toys, paper for drawing, items for craft work, spare clothing for emergencies, etc. These can save a lot of money. When money is required it is helpful to say exactly what it will be used for. People are more likely to respond to the need for ten new chairs or a water tray than to a general request for money for 'equipment'.

Try to be sensitive to the whole church and its needs. You are just one part of a total work but you are always entitled to ask. You may not always receive your requests but try to be understanding and particularly gracious on such occasions. The generosity of our own church at one stage was so great that when the church council were told of our need of funding for playleaders, to our amazement they insisted on giving the money directly, in faith that God would provide the extra through the general giving. He did! We had not asked for money, only for permission to launch a sponsorship scheme in order to raise the necessary funds.

Above all else ask for prayer, otherwise you run the risk of under-resourcing a key part of your work — the spiritual dimension. Follow the suggestions made earlier about producing prayer material for the whole church family. And make sure people know when you meet to pray so that they feel welcome to join you. Some may wish to be part of the prayer chain, especially the elderly and housebound. Occasionally make a point of asking one of the church leaders to attend your prayer meeting.

When the response from our churches is positive let's not fail to say a heartfelt 'thankyou'. It is an encouragement to those who give to know that they are both needed and appreciated. It will also motivate them to continue in that support.

Implementing these suggestions on the key matters of prayer, leadership and church support will involve time and effort. None of them can be achieved overnight. The rapid turnover in leadership and church support will involve time and effort. planning. Increasing numbers of women are returning to work as soon as their children are at full time school, and some even earlier, especially in areas with good nursery provision opportunities for job sharing. This earlier return to work may severely reduce the continuity of leadership and can be very frustrating. At these times we need to remind ourselves that the work belongs to God, not us, and his leading is the point of continuity. Temporary closure of a group or a reduction in the number of activities does not mean failure. God does not stop working and we must pray that he will call others as workers.

It is my personal prayer that God will call many to stay in the work of under fives ministry for longer than just those few pre-school years. So much can be achieved where there is greater continuity in leadership and the build-up of expertise which this brings as well as the tremendous privilege of seeing God work over longer periods of time.

As leaders and workers in under fives groups it is important that we learn to recognise all that God is doing. We can at times fall into the trap of attempting to quantify results in human terms. It may be helpful for us to stop and ask ourselves: exactly how do we evaluate our work?

6.16 How do we evaluate our work?
A few years ago when visiting a church with my husband I asked the vicar if there was any work amongst the under fives and parents. The reply came, 'Well, yes, there is and I suppose they're coming on — they've managed to get one or two into church.'

I delved a little further only to discover that this church had an enormous playgroup, a parent and toddler group bursting at the seams, festival pram services and a mothers' discussion group!

And according to their vicar they were just 'coming on'. Those Christian women were probably in contact with more parishioners than any other group in the church.

This whole conversation made me think more seriously about the way in which we evaluate God's work. Clearly this vicar limited success to those who came to services. I began to wonder how God sees our work. How does he evaluate what we do? If after all our efforts people still don't respond, have we failed? When families come along year after year and enjoy the pleasant and safe surroundings that we provide but seemingly show no more interest in God at the end of it all, have we failed? What of those who occasionally attend the festival services but resist any further personal involvement or interest — have we failed? And then there are those who profess faith but whose families are angry and discourage them — have we failed them?

For every story that we consider a 'success' there must be ten 'failure' stories. But my guess is that we don't see what God sees. Only God could see the success of that first Good Friday. To the disciples and others it was devastating! We are quick to recall the many who believed through their healing and other personal encounters with Jesus. Sometimes I wonder about the nine lepers who didn't return to say thankyou and the rich young ruler who went away sad. What of the thousands that Jesus fed and taught the truths of the Kingdom to — did they all believe and follow Him? We do not know. Perhaps it is not our place to know. But what we do know is that Jesus and his disciples still gave of themselves so that they all heard the message of the Kingdom of God and had the opportunity to respond to it.

There will be many times when we look around our under fives groups and wonder what, if anything, we have achieved. There will be those who have very obviously come to faith and commitment. But there will be many more that we will never know about. We may never see the fruits of our labours.

We cannot dictate to the Holy Spirit how or when he will

work. I believe that God looks for our faithfulness and obedience, not quantified results. He sees us serving our communities, sharing our faith and challenging people with the message of the Kingdom, and thankfully he sees quite clearly the work of his Spirit. Our responsibility is to cooperate with him, not dictate in advance the results we want to see.

The image that remains precious to me from my early days in under fives groups is that of a lighted candle in the darkness and the words 'Thy kingdom come' above it. We are God's lights shining out into the dark world, drawing people to the heart of its message. Through our under fives groups, we have the privilege and opportunity to be part of the work of God. Let's thank him and continue in faithfulness and obedience, entrusting the 'results' to him.

7

Resources for
the Work

This chapter gives details of producers and suppliers of books, leaflets, magazines and audio-visual aids, and the names of supportive organisations and groups, all of which provide useful resources for under fives groups.

Over the last three years I have been involved in many CPAS training events for leaders of under fives groups. As well as providing teaching and workshop training we try to display as many different kinds of resources for the work as is possible. These range from information leaflets, publicity samples and birthday cards, to tapes, puppets and books. Many who have attended these events have shown appreciation for information on how to obtain these resources. Apart from books, which can usually be purchased from any good Christian bookshop, most items have to be ordered or hired from their individual producers and suppliers. Trying to obtain the correct addresses and telephone numbers can be an arduous task. I hope that the following list of organisations and suppliers and the lists of books, tapes and other resources will make the process easier. Where possible I have tried to give specific details on the resources and in some cases suggestions on how they might be used. The majority of items have been referred to in the preceding chapters.

7.1 Names and addresses of support organisations

Pre-School Playgroups Association (PPA)
61–63 Kings Cross Road

London WC1X 9LL
071 833 0991

PPA is a secular organisation providing a wealth of supportive literature on all aspects of playgroup administration, play activities, special interests, publicity and stationery. They are also concerned for parent and toddler groups. Local and national training events are available for leaders of both playgroups and parent and toddler groups. A full list of their publications and details of regional offices can be obtained from the above address. *Under 5's* and *Contact* are two magazines produced by PPA.

Church Pastoral Aid Society (CPAS)
Athena Drive
Tachbrook Park
Warwick CV34 6NG
0926 334242

CPAS is an Anglican home missionary society committed to evangelism, training, and the support of workers in the local church. A wide range of resources are available through their sales unit, many of which are recommended below. Many audio-visual resources can be hired. CPAS have a particular concern for young families and produce an annual pack called 'Families and Under Fives'. A free catalogue containing details of this and other resources is available from the above address.

Scripture Union
130 City Road
London EC1V 2NJ
071 250 1966

Scripture Union is an international interdenominational society. There are over 25 SU bookshops in Britain where all of their publications and audio-visual resources can be purchased. Many of the shops also offer a hiring facility. All items are available through mail order (enquiry number 0272 771131). The hiring of videos and soundstrips is from SU Hire Orders, 9–11, Clothier Road, Brislington, Bristol BS4 5RL.

The Mother's Union
24 Tufton Street
London SW1P 3RD
071 222 5533

The Mother's Union is an Anglican society specially concerned with all that strengthens and preserves marriage and Christian family life. Social concern for young families in society generally is a high priority for the MU and they actively support many inner city projects involving families and pre-school children. Details of local and national activities, publications and training events can be obtained from the above address.

CARE
53 Romney Street
London
SW1P 3RF

CARE aims to promote biblical and Christian action, research and education in order to support the integrity of the family, the centrality of marriage, and the sanctity of human life from conception. Through resources, seminars and training events CARE seeks to encourage and equip Christians in practical caring initiatives within their local community. *CARE News* is a quarterly publication available from the above address. Details of all national and local activities can be found in this magazine.

7.2 Groups offering support for single-parent families
Most under fives groups will include single-parent families. There are a number of national organisations that exist to support and encourage families in these circumstances. Many of these parents will be reluctant to search out such support

groups and so it can be a great help if the information is made readily available through their playgroup or toddler group. Here are some of these organisations and details of the type of service that they provide.

Christian Link Association for Single Parents (CLASP)
Linden
Shorter Avenue
Shenfield
Brentwood
Essex CM15 8RE
0277 233848

CLASP is a Christian organisation which seeks primarily to give support to Christian single parents. It issues a quarterly newsletter and links up parents in the same geographical areas to form local support groups.

National Council for One-Parent Families (NCOPF)
225 Kentish Town Road
London NW5 2LX
071 267 1361

NCOPF is a secular organisation which offers a wide range of free advice and literature to individuals and groups. There are a number of ways of joining NCOPF, from individual membership as a single parent to general group membership. You do not need to be a single parent group in order to be affiliated. *One Parent Times* is the quarterly publication available from the above address. NCOPF do not provide an advice service or local support groups but do, in some areas, set up pre-employment 'back to work' courses.

The Gingerbread Association
35 Wellington Street
London WC2E 7BN
071 267 1361

Gingerbread is a secular organisation which produces a quarterly newspaper and sets up regional groups offering on-going support and encouragement to single parents. Details of membership and local groups can be obtained from the above address.

7.3 Organisations working with Asians
In Contact Ministries
St. Andrew's Road
Plaistow
London E13 8QD

In Contact Ministries specialises in work among the Asian and other ethnic communities in inner city areas of Britain. It is concerned for evangelism and caring, and provides training for those working in these areas. Conferences and training courses are held at the St Andrew's Centre and in churches throughout the country. In Contact also have information about all other societies and churches working in Asian and other ethnic communities throughout Britain.

CLC Asian Literature Department
51 The Dean
Alresford
Hampshire
SO24 9BJ

A range of Christian literature including tracts and Gospels are available in a number of Asian languages.

7.4 Publicity and communication
Christian Publicity Organisation (CPO)
Garcia Estate
Canterbury Rd
Worthing
West Sussex BD13 1BW
0903 64556

On request CPO will send their catalogue and samples of their materials. You can also be placed on their mailing list to receive samples of new materials and the annual catalogue.

Palm Tree Press
Rattlesden
Bury St Edmunds
Suffolk IP30 O52

The Instant Art series of books are ideal for assisting the production of DIY publicity, newsletters and magazines. These are available in most Christian bookshops.

7.5 Producers and suppliers of videos

Many local Christian bookshops are outlets for the sale of Christian videos. Some offer a hiring service. An increasing number of national organisations are making hiring facilities available through mail order. The procedure is simple and in most cases inexpensive, making videos more accessible to Christians engaged in evangelistic work. Here are three organisations which offer this hiring service:

Gospel Vision
143 Toller Lane
Bradford
West Yorkshire BD89 9HL
0274 54137

Christian World Centre
Box 30
123 Deansgate
Manchester M60 3BX
061 834 6060

International Films
235 Shaftesbury Ave
London
071 836 2255

A list giving full details of films is available at each of these centres. Orders can be taken by telephone and will be posted directly to you. In most cases videos are returnable within seven days.

Other producers of videos previously mentioned include:

Bagster Video
76 High Street
Alton
Hants GU34 1EN
0420 89141

Sunrise Video
P O Box 814
Worthing
West Sussex BN11 1TS

London Bible College
Green Lane
Northwood
Middlesex
HA6 2UW

7.6 Resources for training in personal evangelism

Many Christians are lacking in confidence and skills when it comes to the sharing of their faith. There are a number of good courses available designed specifically for encouraging and equipping individuals in the task of personal evangelism. They include:

Care to Say Something by Scripture Union. A study book designed to help Christians talk freely about their faith.

Operation Breakthrough by CPAS is the complete self-help training course in evangelism. Whilst originally designed for teenagers, it has been successfully used across all age groups in local churches.

What I've Always Wanted to Say by CPAS is concerned with personal witness and designed to give individuals confidence and to help them with the basic skills of expressing their faith.

7.7 Evangelistic materials for use with adults
Christian Foundations, CPAS

Jesus Then and Now, Lion (available through CPAS).

Good News Down The Street, CPAS.

SEAN, Allen Gardiner House, Penbury Road, Tunbridge Wells, Kent TN2 3QU. Ask for the *Young Parents Leader's Manual* to be used with this course.

All of these are suitable for one-to-one or small group work. They come complete with outlines and discussion material. For further details and suggestions on how they might be used, refer back to chapter 5.5.

Warren Norman, *Journey Into Life*, Kingsway (available through CPAS).

CPO — a wide range of topical leaflets and tracts available (address above).

7.8 Useful magazines

Christian Family
Elm House
New Malden
Surrey KT3 3HB
081 942 9761

Home and Family (Mother's Union)
The Mary Sumner House
24 Tufton Street
London
SW1P 3RB
071 222 5533

Christian Woman
Herald House
Dominion Road
Worthing
West Sussex
BN14 8JP

7.9 Useful reading for leaders of playgroups and parent and toddler groups

Lucas and Henderson, *Pre-School Playgroups, A Handbook*, Allen and Unwin.
Donoghue, Joyce, *Running a Mother and Toddler Club*, Unwin.
Sheridon, Mary, *From Birth to Five Years*, NFER Nelson.
Wyatt, Grace, *Charnwood*, Lion.
Porter, David, *Children at Risk*, Kingsway.
Porter, David, *Children at Play*, Kingsway.

7.10 Reading and resources for leading children in worship

These resources are particularly relevant to chapters 3 and 4.
Bridger, Francis, *Children Finding Faith*, SU.
Buckland, Ron, *Children and God*, SU.
Children in the Way, Church House Publishing.
Durran, Maggie, *All Age Worship*, Angel Press.
Stevenson, Elspeth, *Tell It to Jesus*, SU.
When you Pray with 3–6's, NCEC.
Lush, Michael, *Know How — all-age activities for learning in worship*, SU.
Mellor, Howard, *Know How — to encourage family worship*, SU.
For All The Family, Ed. Michael Botting, Kingsway.
The Dramatised Bible, Lion (available through CPAS).
The Lion Children's Bible, Lion.
Children's Communion Book, Mowbrays

For music and song tapes, see below.

7.11 Teaching materials for the under fives

These teaching materials were written for use in children's groups such as Sunday schools and pram services. But many of them contain ideas and suggestions that are easily adaptable for all-age family worship.

First Steps — Working with the under fives, Church House Publishing. Ideal for pram service themes.

Pram Service Ideas for Mother's Day, Easter and Harvest — MTYM 9 and 10. Families and Under Fives 1, CPAS.

Learning Together — Under 5's, SU.
Trek for age 3 years upwards, CPAS.

7.12 Visual aids for teaching and worship

Glove Puppet Kits, Celebration Screenprint, PO Box 68, Redhill, Surrey RH1 4YT. Scripts also available.

Families and Under Fives 1, CPAS. Further puppet ideas, scripts and design for a puppet booth.

Help! I can't draw, SU.
Instant Art — Bible Cut-outs, Palm Tree Press.

Bible Story Friezes, NCEC.

Bible Story Friezes, SU.

A full list of children's story books is given below.

7.13 Christian books for children
There is a wealth of good children's literature now available in most Christian bookshops. They range from inexpensive small booklets to beautifully illustrated large hardback books. Many of the cheaper range can be given as suitable birthday, Christmas or leaving gifts whilst others can be bought for use in a book corner or lending library. Nearly every child enjoys a good story

and below is a selection of those that have been well used in various under fives groups. The list is by no means exhaustive.

Scripture Union:

Simon and Sarah Books (4 in the series).
Little Fish Books (over 20 child-size books available in 5 series)
Thank You God For Our Day... (4 in the series).
Shaped Board Books by Pam Mara.
My First Prayer Books (4 in the series).
Miles Books (4 in the series) by Taffy Davies suitable for aged 4 upwards only.
God's World Makes Me Feel So Small by Helen Caswell.

Bible Society:
Talk About books (12 titles).
What the Bible Tells Us (14 titles) age 3 yrs and over.
Colouring Books (9 in the series).

Lion Publishing:
Little Lions (11 in the series).
Lion Story Bible (52 in the series) age 4 yrs and over, also available on video.

Palm Tree Press:
Bible Stories (32 titles).
Palm Tree Children's Bible — New Testament.
Palm Tree Children's Bible — Old Testament.

Marshall Pickering:
Best of the Bunch by Butterworth and Inkpen (4 in the series).
I Wonder by Butterworth and Inkpen (4 in the series)
The Mouse's Story by Butterworth and Inkpen (4 in the series).

The above series of books provide excellent storytelling material for pram services — with very attractive illustrations.

Hodder and Stoughton:
>   *The Nativity Play* by Butterworth and Inkpen.
>   *First Bible Stories* (4 in the series).

7.14 Books that may help children through difficult times

The arrival of a new baby into a family, the death of a close friend or relative, separation or divorce of parents, the death of a pet, or fear of the dark, are all very stressful for a child. Here are a selection of children's books that may help both parent and child through these difficult times. It can be useful to have these titles available in a resource or lending library in your under-fives group.

Alex, M & B, *Grandpa and Me*, Lion.

Varley, Susan, *Badger's Parting Gift*, Collins.

A Benjamin book, *The Day Grandma Died*, Church House Publications.

Hughes, Jeremy, *Will My Rabbit Go To Heaven?* Lion.

Smith and Graham, *Jenny's Baby Brother*, A Picture Lion.

Hoban, Russell, *A Baby Sister for Francis*, Puffin.

Hutchins, Pat, *Goodnight, Owl*, Puffin.

Tomlinson, Jill, *The Owl Who Was Afraid of the Dark*, Puffin.

Baum, Louis, *Are We Nearly There?* Magnet.

Two helpful adults books related to two of the above problem areas are:

Wynnejones, Pat, *Children, Death and Bereavement*, SU.

Swihart and Brigham, *Helping Children of Divorce*, SU.

7.15 Music books and tapes suitable for children

Shephard, Margaret, *Music with Mum*, PPA.

Playgroup Music, PPA.

Nursery Children Sing, Scripture Press. 120 songs and action rhymes with simple melodies and easy words, specially for 2's and 3's.

Let's Sing! Songs for 4's and 5's, Scripture Press. Music book and accompanying cassette available.

God Is For Me, Fisherfolk sing songs for children. Cassette tape.

Come and Sing, SU. Music and word book.

Come and Sing Some More, SU.

Sing to God, SU. Music and word book.

Kids Praise, Psalm tapes and other children's praise tapes. Maranatha Music.

Jesus Loves Me, available from CPAS.

Sing to the King, available from Sutton, 10 Wellington Rd, St Albans AL1 5NL.

Come and Praise. Music and word book, BBC Publications.

7.16 Further resources for use with individuals and in groups

Caring for New Christians, SU and Bible Society.

Square One, CPAS. Baptism preparation kit.

One To Five. Pre-School Christian Nurture pack available from Rev S. Swidenbank, Flat 1, 'Engadine', New Road, Windermere, Cumbria LA23 2LA.

Little People 1, 2 & 3. Three video presentations following the development of a child's personality from 0–5 years. Available from London Bible College, Green Lane, Northwood, Middlesex HA6 2UW.

7.17 Further books related to working with under fives and families

Hattam, John, *Family Evangelism*, SU.

Keay, Kathy, *Women to Women*, MARC/EA. An excellent book looking at a wide range of different women's experiences of reaching other women.

Together with Under Fives, Church House Publishing. A resource anthology.

Crawford, Kathleen, *Under Fives Welcome!* SU. An invaluable reference book containing practical ideas and suggestions on how churches can develop their children's work.

Whitehouse, Carl, *Families on the Way*, SU. A Christian doctor looks at some of the questions and difficulties that parents face when wanting children. These include problems in conception, adoption, bereavement and child handicaps.